The Amazing Story of Airbnb

A Successful Silicon Valley Startup that Changed the World

By
Edward White

© **Copyright 2019 - All rights reserved.**

The content contained within this book may not be reproduced, duplicated or transmitted without direct written permission from the author or the publisher.

Under no circumstances will any blame or legal responsibility be held against the publisher, or author, for any damages, reparation, or monetary loss due to the information contained within this book. Either directly or indirectly.

Legal Notice:

This book is copyright protected. This book is only for personal use. You cannot amend, distribute, sell, use, quote or paraphrase any part, or the content within this book, without the consent of the author or publisher.

Disclaimer Notice:

Please note the information contained within this document is for educational and entertainment purposes only. All effort has been executed to present accurate, up to date, and reliable, complete information. No warranties of any kind are declared or implied. Readers acknowledge that the author is not engaging in the rendering of legal, financial, medical or professional advice. The content within this book has been derived from various sources. Please consult a licensed professional before attempting any techniques outlined in this book.

By reading this document, the reader agrees that under no circumstances is the author responsible for any losses, direct or indirect, which are incurred as a result of the use of information contained within this document, including, but not limited to, — errors, omissions, or inaccuracies.

Table of Contents

Introduction 1
Chapter 1: Ascension 6
Chapter 2: Attaining Investments 17
    Breakfast in Bread 24
    Thanks, Obama! 27
    Cereal Killers 31
    New York, New York 37
Chapter 3: After Initial Revenue 41
    Growth Phase 47
    A Matter of Trust 49
    When the Going Gets Tough 54
    Enter the Lobbyists 60
    The Art of Being Popular 61
    Weighing the Scales 64
Chapter 4: And In Recent Beginnings 67
    When the Price is Nice 70
    Return of the Brand 72
    Nomads on the Run 76
    The Hosts 79
    The Business of the Host 83
    The Horror! 84
    Keeping Things Safe 87

When Things Are beyond Control _____ 91

The Law of the Land _____ 95

The Copycats _____ 106

New York, New York _____ 109

Do You Want To Be a Host? _____ 114

Mark Your Scars and Get Back In the Fight _____ 118

A Home Away From Home _____ 121

VRBO for You? _____ 123

Leveling the Playing Field _____ 123

Chapter 5: Management Styles _____ 127

Mentorship _____ 129

Chapter 6: The Future of Airbnb _____ 131

Togetherness _____ 132

A Billion is Not a Big Number Right? _____ 133

Airbnb Collections _____ 134

Airbnb Types _____ 135

Airbnb Plus and Beyond by Airbnb _____ 136

Success! _____ 138

Airbnb and its Customers _____ 142

Here is Some Advice _____ 145

The Three Musketeers _____ 145

Conclusion _____ 147

Bibliography _____ 148

Introduction

You need a place to stay.

Not right now of course. You are most likely within the comfort of your home. Or you could be reading this book on the subway or in your office.

However, you might need a place to stay when you are traveling.

You would possibly look through the hotels in the country, city, or area you are visiting. You might compare them to other hotel rooms. You might ask yourself a dozen questions (maybe more) about your room choices.

Does this hotel (or any other type of accommodation) fit my traveling budget?

Does it have WiFi so that I can stay connected or maybe upload my pictures and videos?

Does it come with free breakfast? Because if I get to enjoy a free meal in the morning, I might as well skip paying for dinner and spend more on drinks. Definitely sounds like a tempting idea.

Will I be able to receive good service? Perhaps I should check the reviews of this place and see what others think of it.

And those are just some of the questions you are going to ask yourself about your temporary place of stay. From cleanliness to the food, from the availability of parking space (hey, who knows?) to the distance from the airport, you might have many criteria to pick your hotel.

Looking through the hotel rooms available to you, the choices might seem to lie in two categories; expensive rooms that meet your tastes or cheaper alternatives with perhaps questionable quality.

So what do you do then? What if you wanted to spend as little as possible on your housing because you wanted to experience the location, the sights or even the local eateries? What if your main priority was not the place you are sleeping in but the places you are planning on visiting? But at the same time, you do not want to pick any room in order to make a quick decision. You want something comfortable and, preferably, clean.

Earlier, you might have had to simply sigh in defeat and pick one of the choices you already have. After all, there are no alternatives are there? You begrudgingly decide to get one of the options that are available. No point overthinking it right now.

Today, you might not have to experience such disappointments.

By simply using an app, you have the option of choosing between a myriad of homes, apartments, guesthouses, bunk beds, trailer trucks, camps, and so much more. You can compare prices between them. You can look at the interiors. You can see if you get any additional features. Some even show you what kind of food they offer.

None of these temporary abodes are under the ownership or management of hotels.

Real people, who decided to rent out these spaces to traveler, own all of these rooming or resting spaces. Some of the spots are owned by families, giving away a part of their homes (their actual homes mind you) temporarily to tourists and traveler. Others are properties managed by individuals, hoping to earn a little extra money on the side.

Now there is a benefit to all this, which we shall look at further.

But the point of the matter is that you are not limited by options, prices, or availability. You do not have to worry about missing the best rooms for the night in your chosen destination. You do not have to check your bank balance and perform multiple calculations about your spend just to find appropriate lodgings.

You can completely focus on your holiday and your trip.

In fact, your stay might be an experience in itself.

Do you want to experience living in a cozy tent overlooking some magnificent vistas? You have the option to do that. Do you feel like living inside a mobile trailer the way you have seen people do in the movies? Just book it for a specific period and you are good to go. Do you want to stay in a place that provides you with all the amenities of a decent hotel at half the price? Well, you have to look no further.

With such unique places to temporary settle in, your travel plans might just end up being much better than you had originally conceived.

You simply head over to a website or app and choose your destination. The results you see after your selection will present you with enough choices for homestays that your biggest concern is not the lack of options, but the abundance of it. You might be spoilt for choices and making a decision might not be easy.

However, you can enjoy that comfort today thanks to an idea conceived by two unemployed youngsters who simply wanted to earn a little extra cash.

Today, their idea is a multi-billion dollar brand that has reshaped the hotel industry. In fact, hotels are now investing in alternative options that offer budget-friendly stays with additional experiences.

Take the renown brand Marriott for example. They understand the benefits that Airbnb is providing to its users. In turn, they wanted to offer their own unique services to compete with the ones provided by Airbnb. They started Moxy, their subsidiary that offers reasonably priced communal rooms. These rooms are connected to communal services and areas such as bars, parks, restaurants, and entertainment areas.

Marriott knows that Airbnb offers more than just budget-friendly rooms that are distinct, comfortable, and memorable.

- Rooms you book on Airbnb are an experience of their own. Every moment of your travel might have something for you to remember.

- As many lodgings on the platform are under the ownership of local people, you receive wonderful insights into the community, location hotspots, travel guides and tips, essential services, and more. The best part? You might get them all for free.

- Because anyone has the opportunity to open up their homes for tourists, Airbnb provides homestays dispersed across the country, some close to your location of interest. With this freedom of choice, you can stay at one spot and then shift to another, depending on your preference.

- You can choose a place to stay using wide selection features. What if you are traveling to Thailand but you would like your host to speak English? Sure, make a quick search using the language filter. Do you need certain amenities that are essential for your experience? No problem, you have the filters for that.

- If you are a host, Airbnb provides you the convenience of setting a price for the room or space you would like to rent out. You can fix a daily, weekly, or monthly price. This gives you better means of earning through the platform and your guests have the freedom to choose the duration that best fits their needs. Everyone comes out a winner.

Providing each traveler the ability to make the choice for their stay or each host the option to promote their homes in the same platform works for many people. Think of it link an eBay for travel lodgings; forget the intermediaries and hidden fees.

All of this sounds incredible. But before a surge of excitement compels you to download the app and begin using it, you should know more about how this company started, the pitfalls it had to face during its development phase, and the situation it is in currently.

That is what you will know and understand in the coming chapters.

The account of the life of Airbnb.

Chapter 1: Ascension

Let us journey back in time to the year 2015. Frankly, it's a short journey. And no, this is not the year when Airbnb was launched. The launch occurred much earlier.

However, during this year (and shortly before Thanksgiving), Airbnb raised nearly $100 million. While that amount might sound big, it was a pittance compared to the sum that they had raised earlier, during the same year (that sum was an astounding $1.5 billion.) Just for reference, the total GDP of Dominica was a little more than $496 million in 2017.

So yes, it was an incredible amount to raise by a company that was valued at nearly $25.5 billion.

Yes, at that point, they were riding the carriage of success. They utilize the number of nights booked as a metric for success and, based on their information, they had hit 78 million nights in the year 2015.

According to sources, that was nearly double the number of nights booked in 2014. And that was just the beginning of their success.

Now let us travel further back in time, to the year 2010.

The company had gained some buzz. Tech magazines began to notice the arrival of Airbnb on their radars. They ran pieces about the up-and-company hospitality brand that was creating quite a few disruptions, especially in their offerings of cheap lodgings for people.

But industry experts were still skeptical. In their minds, Airbnb still created an impression of "these guys?" rather than "oh, it is these guys!" They had not made a significant mark.

Why would they? After all, it was not as if their idea was unique. Not at all. You had companies such as HomeAway, Couchsurfing and even a brand named, similar to Airbnb, BedandBreakfast who all provided the service of hosting homes.

So what can this company offer that none of its predecessors are already providing to the masses? What difference can they make? How can they take over the market dominated by brands that have established themselves already?

It seemed as though Airbnb would never make a mark or create a difference.

Nevertheless, a difference is what they made.

In fact, they did not just make a difference. They became different themselves.

Like the other sites, they started out by listing rooms for rent provided by different hosts. Soon, the hosts started displaying unique housing spaces. Treehouses, boats, and camping tents were just some of the offerings you could find on Airbnb. That made them a topic of conversation. This eventually attracted the millennials, who were eager to try out new homes that were both affordable and adventurous. You had a platform that could provide unconventional places to stay hosted by like-minded people at room rates cheaper than a hotel room. That was enough to be a selling point for many people.

Their listings began to increase.

Along with that, their bookings caught fire. Not literally. What I meant was that their bookings were increasing at a rapid rate.

Before long it was the year 2011. They had managed to raise nearly $112 million from investors. Not a paltry amount to claim from a company that had just recently established itself in the market. It was then valued at an amount slightly north of a billion dollars. It had successfully received more than a million bookings on its platform.

However, during the years that follow, those numbers would mean nothing.

They were set to accomplish more.

Their bookings increased from a million to five million. From there, the numbers began to rise faster: increasing to 10, 40, and eventually reaching more than 120 million bookings in the year 2016. It was not just their bookings that were affected. The valuation of the company began to climb over the years as well. Airbnb went from being valued at a billion dollars to 10 billion dollars. From there, its value increased to nearly $25 billion dollars in the year 2015.

Today, Airbnb has a value of nearly $38 billion dollars.

While that sounds like a lot, it still does not explain the entire potential of Airbnb. There are many houses left to explore and numerous hosts still signing up on the platform.

When looking at the growth of Airbnb, one feels a tremendous sense of awe. We understand that the idea was practically simple. I mean, if only you or I could have discovered it earlier, we would be riding the billion-dollar horse right now. That does sound like the dream. Though any dream requires more than just an idea. It needs the assistance of luck and the right timing.

Airbnb has both of those factors:

- It came out at the right time, following the great recession that shook the world in 2008. As the housing market was plummeting, people were able to make money out of their homes. This also presented tourists with an affordable means of travel It became a win-win situation for the buyer and seller.

- The millennials were already looking for new and innovative things in the market. It was lucky that they found Airbnb and it was additional luck that homeowners began listing unique forms of property on the platform.

The average earnings between Airbnb hosts in the year 2015 was twice the amount they paid on their rent.

This is what helped boost Airbnb's revenue: they were offering benefits to all the parties involved in the transaction and allowing the feature of creative spaces on the platform.

What Airbnb succeeded at was not merely the benefits they offered to their hosts, but the unique and different experiences they were offering to traveler. This, compounded with their ability to offer inexpensive options, worked well to speed their growth. Even those homes that featured imperfections began to seem like unique places to live in. They embodied cultures and traditions that traveler from around the world wanted to include as part of their journey. This opened up access to new areas, locales, and neighborhoods. You could encounter the lives of the locals, living as they do and viewing the location from their perspective. Instead of always using popular tourist attractions, you could experience something unique. The houses listed on Airbnb themselves became a means to explore more!

This particularly resonated with the millennials, who were embracing the culture of exploring the roads less traveled. Additionally, as connectivity was becoming a greater influence in our lives, it was no surprise that millennials - who connected with people online - would not be bothered to live in the homes of the people they had connected with online. Let's face it. The idea appealed to us all. I know I used Airbnb a lot during my travels and quite frankly, I still do.

While all the benefits of Airbnb with regards to the experiences it allowed people to go through were exceptional, there was another factor that came into play; human connection.

Think about this. You are renting a space in someone's home. You are living in the home for the duration of your stay (or however long you had decided to book the room.) You live through their routines and their habits. You actually get to connect with these people. There is a sense of intimacy that one cannot easily express unless they have lived in a stranger's home.

If the person is physically present in the home, you can interact with them. You get to know more about them. They become part of your stories and you become part of theirs. This allowed a degree of human bonding that enhanced your traveling experience.

Even if the host was not present in the house during your stay, you still understand the fact that they had prepared the space for you. It becomes a personal feeling.

You might recollect its slogan (or you may not, which is alright); "travel like a human."

That is what made Airbnb unique. It was not merely about

ticking off items on your bucket list. It was having a truly human experience in an unfamiliar place.

In a world where most people have their sights on the device in front of them, their hearing focused on the tunes booming from their earbud, or their existence isolated, whether physically or mentally, Airbnb has the ability to provide the human connection that we often seek.

That does not mean that there are no downfalls. Of course, with a business model like Airbnb's, there are bound to be disasters sprinkled along the company's path to progress. This arrives in the form of governments and municipalities of countries proclaiming that individuals allowing their homes, rooms or other spaces to be rented out to other individuals in illegal. The laws established by the governments and municipalities are not the same everywhere, but they possessed the same underlying idea; they wanted to curb the disruption caused by Airbnb on local housing and hospitality industries. In short, Airbnb was a threat. The more the company grew, the stronger the opposition became. Proponents of this opposition claimed that Airbnb affected local properties and housing businesses. Additionally, the hosts who allow traveler to stay within their spaces do not pay taxes. While Airbnb clearly states the inclusion of taxes in their systems based on the country of the host, it seems that government officials are unable to record these transactions properly, leading to much debate and confusion.

Municipal corporations have complaints about the noise levels of the occupants of Airbnb homes. Each city has its own regulations regarding rest hours. In numerous cities around the world, noise levels should not exceed a certain decibel beyond a specific time. In some cities like Prague, loud noises are not allowed between the hours of 10:00 p.m. and 6:00

a.m. Failure to comply with these rules might lead to law enforcement intervening to control the situation.

The company has also faced problems from the hosts and traveler as well. Ransacking, thefts, property damages, and even physical attacks against hosts and their lodgings were some of the difficulties that plagued the company. Numerous hosts were also behind some of the problems caused through the platform. Racial discrimination from the hosts occurred to many occupants. Additionally, the lack of responsibility among the hosts caused unintended harm to traveler during their stay.

These harms are perhaps a reflection of the society or the local community. Misusing the platform and abusing the trust of the user is not a highlight of the platform itself, but of individuals. However, the damage was caused by the company's reputation. Airbnb may not have been the proponents of the disasters faced by traveler and hosts, but they were certainly facing the brunt of the devastation to their reputation.

Soon, news began to spread about the situations faced on Airbnb. There were articles written about them. In fact, you could actually perform an internet search on "scary experiences on Airbnb" and chances are that you might find an "X Airbnb Stories That You Won't Believe Are True" kind of article.

Bad news definitely spreads fast.

These negative information began to create a panic among the masses, especially to those who haven't made use of the platform yet and their only source of information about the company was the news.

Much of these incidents occur because Airbnb has made an easy-to-use and easy-to-access platform that allows hosts to display their properties in their own way. This means hosts decide to capture pictures of their homes, highlighting its features and even talk about nearby amenities. This allows hosts to create superficial presentations of their homes.

However, with each new problem comes a solution. Airbnb is now regulating the media and information that goes into the system. They have allowed for paying travelers to form a community by rating and reviewing the homes they visit. The verified ID system allows for them to include only those homes that have been verified by the system.

All these changes showed the company's resiliency to answer some of the common misconceptions about the platform. While they did manage to dissipate some grievances among the masses, they were still able to excite those who were concerned about its functions.

Regardless, the company grew.

One of the major factors responsible for their success was that the properties listed on their platform were also urban. With many hotels, you often find that they are located in the most exotic locations, or in the financial or residential hub of a city. There are of course exceptions - with options scattered throughout the city - but often their quality is questionable at best. But Airbnb allowed people to turn urban spaces into temporary housing for travelers.

The majority of the listings on Airbnb are studio, one-bedroom, and two-bedroom apartments. This makes it an instant hit among the millennials and many travelers (and a threat to hotels.) These apartment listings gave diversity to the options available on Airbnb; you could find a place to stay that matched your tastes. The urban stays were modern, many, and it had enough of the "millennial" touch to make it popular among modern travelers.

That's not all. Airbnb also offered the users that listed their property on their site the chance to post their listings on Craigslist, an online classifieds platform. It gave Airbnb millions of potential users who could access the listing from the classifieds platform (especially in those countries where Craigslist was popular.) The ability to make the listings appear much better and more professional attracted the Craigslist market from the unorganized, sometimes unclean and quite often shady looking listings they had to typically deal with.

In any online business, the ability to scale faster (and better) makes all the difference. Airbnb were able to reach a substantial size in their operations and reach because they were able to scale in unique ways. They took advantage of every opportunity presented to them (case in point: Craigslist.) That ability of Airbnb to capitalize on opportunities allowed it to reach a level of dominance that was difficult to topple. And tricky to ban in every country.

You see, regardless of how certain countries in the world viewed the services offered by Airbnb, it was still creating a massive influx of tourists. More tourists meant more businesses and revenue to the country. This was not an easy factor to overlook, particularly for those countries that rely on tourism to earn a portion of their income.

But a company's growth is not an automatic occurrence. Any company's success and growth rests up on the shoulders of those piloting it. For the founders of Airbnb, there was much they had to learn and experience to bring the brand to the position it enjoys today.

As the company grew, there were noticeable changes in the founders as well. No, they did not separate, which is typically what happens to the founders of many tech companies. Brian Chesky, Joe Gebbia, and Nathan Blecharczyk are still the captains of the Airbnb ship. They continue to manage its affairs, its innovations, and other factors of its growth. They have learned much from their experiences to be the leaders they are now. However, it was not always the case.

You see, the three founders had a lack of corporate experience when they first launched the company. Well, it was actually Chesky and Gebbia who had launched the company and they roped in Blecharczyk as the third founder after the first week. However, the fact remains. None of these guys had experience managing a company or a team. They had to learn everything on the fly.

In fact, Chesky had limited knowledge about investors, businesses, and website construction beyond the creation of a basic web platform. Despite the lack of knowledge and experience, Chesky had to evolve himself from starting an online listing platform to managing a billion dollar company with thousands of employees.

Of course, the other two founders each had to learn and evolve in their own way. Gebbia had a knack for displaying bold ideas and presenting entrepreneurial skills. Blecharczyk was known to be a talented software designer who is responsible for building the foundations that Airbnb was built on. Even today, much of the infrastructure of the platform is in existence thanks to his ingenuity and skills.

Together, they have managed to build a brand into a success story. Even now, their journey has not ended.

Airbnb is constantly evolving. It has added the ability to search for experiences for its users, allowing travelers to enjoy unique and popular activities by booking them directly on the platform. The company soon wants to expand into restaurant reservations and land transportation. Plans also include the expansion into an idea involving flights that they have not expounded up on in much detail.

Airbnb is definitely growing; there is no doubt about that. But with more growth comes bigger challenges. There are more legal battles the company might have to face and more problems that need fixing. There might definitely be more human-created horror scenarios that the founders have no control over but that, nevertheless, could cause irreparable damage to their company.

However, whilst the challenges are many, the company has also set in place some remarkable milestones for itself. It has changed the way we book spaces and homes during travels. It has innovated the idea of experience. It has built human connections.

All of this occurred with many odds stacked against the company. Industry experts were not confident about their idea. Investors did not provide the support required to build the company or boost the morale of its founders. Eventually, even the public and the governments of various countries took a stand against the company.

If Chesky, Gebbia, and Blecharczyk had called it quits, then perhaps there wouldn't be a platform that not only changed the way we tra, but the way we interacted with other people.

The ascension of Airbnb might have been strong, but there is a big story behind its success; one that can serve to inspire those who find it difficult to battle against the odds.

Chapter 2: Attaining Investments

The story of how Chesky and Gebbia started Airbnb is already the stuff of legends. The founders have landed themselves in the hall of fame of other success stories; those of legendary founders like Jeff Bezos – who started Amazon as an online bookstore – or Steve Jobs – who was a college dropout with dreams of changing the way people used computers. You might have read it somewhere but for those who have not discovered this success story, here is an introduction into it.

The year was 2007. Two art school graduates found themselves unemployed. That brought in numerous troubles for the lads. Most particularly, they needed to find a way to earn some money. They were living together in a three-bedroom apartment and they needed the money for the rent.

A design conference – named the International Council of Societies of Industrial Design World Congress - that was making its way into the city was the opportunity they were looking for. The event would be attracting at least a couple of thousand attendees. Chesky and Gebbia know that nearby hotels would all be nearly booked and the rates of available rooms would be high. They needed to make a move quickly.

After discovering that all the nearby hotel rooms were indeed booked, the duo decided to rent out the empty space in the apartment to anyone who would require it.

Fortunately, Gebbia happened to have three air mattresses that were reminders of a campaign trip he had taken.

That created a wonderful space for the would-be temporary room renters; they would have a bedroom, separate bathroom, and even a kitchen. Chesky and Gebbia could rent out the pace at a cheap price. In fact, they thought of even offering breakfast.

The plan was set and they were ready to rent out the apartment.

But coming up with the idea was only the beginning of the process. They need to find out just how to advertise the apartment to potential lodgers and more importantly. Just where to place the listing.

Two ideas blossomed into their minds.

- They would advertise the space on design blogs and websites that they knew the attendees of the conference would be reading.

- They would create a website to list the room.

They now had a plan. All they needed to do now was to execute it. Realizing that the deadline for the room rent was close, Chesky and Gabbia knew they had nothing to lose. They had just one option and that was to dive into the implementation of their new idea and hope for the best.

And that is what they did.

They refined their idea over the course of weeks, noticing the ever-looming presence of their rent situation. They began to plan wireframes and mockups for the website that would feature their room. They hired a freelancer who would put together a website based on the duo's designs. When it came to naming the service, Chesky and Gebbia chose AirBed & Breakfast.

They got in touch with the conference organizers and numerous online design portals to advertise their website, who were glad to help.

The website was ready. The advertising of the service was well under way. The price for the bed space was fixed at $80 per night, including all amenities and breakfast.

Now came the waiting game.

Chesky and Gebbia were not hoping for much. They would be satisfied with even a couple of backpackers making use of their space. But whatever was supposed to happen had to happen fast. Time was running out and it would not be too long before the landlord came knocking on their door for the rent.

It seemed like the situation was inevitable. They had to move out after all.

That was when they got their first surprise.

A few people had booked their room.

And not just any people.

Amol Surve, an Indian who had graduated from Arizona State University; Michael, a father of five; Kat, a designer from Boston.

These three would be their first guests.

None of them was mere backpackers. They were professionals who were looking for an inexpensive place to stay.

Surve even booked five nights at the room, giving Chesky and Gebbia a breathing space for their rental situation. The match was perfect; the guests were looking to cut down on their costs —which would not be possible had they chosen the hotels in the area - and the Chesky and Gebbia were looking to use whatever they could earn for the rent.

Soon enough, the would-be founders realized that the whole idea of renting out spaces to people was not such a bad idea after all. They might have just stumbled on to something here. Could this be a business opportunity? After all, they were able to pay their rent effectively. Could they not be able to earn more? Perhaps they only needed to add a few more mattresses, a few more rooms, and that group of three guests who had initially used their space could turn to ten.

The only problem was; how are they going to market their idea? Where do they start? Business ventures are expensive and Chesky and Gebbia did not exactly have the resources to start anything on their own. Adding a few more beds would not solve their problem. They would have to wait years before that venture gave them any capital. Plus, let us not forget about the rent.

That was when an idea struck to them; how about the conference itself? They could become one of the attendees and then approach people, and possibly investors, inside the conference.

The idea was sound and preparations were made to attend the conference.

The got in touch with Michael Seibel, co-founder of Justin.tv (which would later go on to become Twitch, the popular streaming site for gamers around the world). He told them that he would get them in touch with "angel investors."

So before we continue on the journey of Airbnb, I thought I should give you a brief primer on Angel Investors. In short, these investors are typically individuals with high net worth. They provide financial assistance to (or in other words, they invest in) businesses in the early stages of the business venture. You may typically find angel investors within the family. However, that is not a rule set in stone. Many angel investors look for a stake in the company, but once again, that might not always be the case.

Back to the story.

What soon followed was not something Chesky and Gebbia had predicted would happen.

As they began to pitch their ideas to people, most of them either were amused or dismissed them entirely. No one gave their idea any consideration. No one was even curious to explore the possibilities of such a venture.

Disappointed, but not entirely dispirited, the duo headed back to their apartment and decided to run through their idea again. Perhaps they were missing something. They needed to brainstorm more and create a well-developed idea. This time, they had the vigor and determination to start their company for real. They wanted to make it happen real badly.

They soon added another member, one of Gebbia's previous roommates named Nathan Blecharczyk.

Blecharczyk was known to be a gifted engineer and had actually made close to $1 million creating software and selling them. He would be a valuable member of the team indeed.

They got together and began the brainstorming ideas.

Their first idea was to create a website where they would be able to match roommates. The idea was that people could go online on their portal and find a roommate with they could share a space. The idea seemed to be a cross between Craigslist and Facebook. However, after spending weeks on the idea and developing it into a workable process, the team checked the URL roommates.com.

They were crushed to discover that someone else had already implemented their idea.

Not ones to give up, they dove straight back into their brainstorming session. They had to come up with something else.

Chesky would often find his thoughts drifting back to the idea of AirBed & Breakfast. After all, it did work when they first launched it. Sure, it wasn't a major success nor did it propel their idea into a business (not to forget the negative feedback they had received from most people at the conference). However, Chesky felt like the team was on to something.

Together with Gebbia, he decided to have a go at the idea once again. Maybe they had too simply refine the idea to add new life into it.

An idea soon struck them; what if they targeted conferences around the country? The first time they launched AirBed & Breakfast, they took advantage of a growing demand for inexpensive lodgings when hotels were hiking their prices.

Perhaps the idea would be the same. They knew that during any major conference, hotels would find themselves completely booked. Those late to find suitable bookings would struggle with rising prices.

Their idea could solve that problem. To the duo, it seemed like the perfect opportunity to attract guests.

In fact, they even knew which conference to target first.

South by Southwest or SXSW, one of the leading consortium

of tech, media, and music conferences and festivals held annually in Austin, Texas. With the number of attendees, they could easily attract more guests to the spaces they would be renting out.

And so, together with Blecharczyk, they developed a website that would be an alternative to expensive hotels.

The last time, they had reached out to design blogs and portals to market their idea. No reason not to try out a similar idea for their latest idea. With that, they reached out to tech portals and sent across some notifications.

Then they waited.

And waited.

Nothing happened.

Eventually, they got only two paying customers.

One of whom was Chesky himself. The other was Tiendung Le, a Ph.D. student who they discovered on Craigslist and recruited him to list his lodging space on AirBed & Breakfast.

But apart from those two, nobody else came to the website or listed their homes. There were zero guests who were interested in using the services of AirBed & Breakfast, definitely a deterioration from their previous listing. This caused the team to think more about their concept.

Despite the fact that they attracted nearly zero business into the platform, they found that they were able to discover some flaws in the system, mainly concerned with the payment mechanics.

After knowing this, the three founders realized two things:

- They would need to refine their idea even more.
- They needed to improve the payment system.

The upside to their whole endeavor was that potential guests contacted them after the completion of the SXSW conference. These guests were not planning to visit any conferences. Rather, they were travelers who needed a place to stay in the city, preferably a place where the rents were not outrageous. They had stumbled across AirBed & breakfast and thought that the idea was rather smart. They eventually contacted the founders and asked them if they were willing to allow the guests to use AirBed & Breakfast.

At this point, you might think that the founders discovered their Eureka moment and said yes to the guess instantly, leading to the formation of Airbnb.

Sadly, that was not to be the case.

Chesky, Gebbia, and Blecharczyk declined the guests, saying they were not interested.

Breakfast in Bread

So their plan did not go as, well, planned.

What can the founders do? What other options do they have at this time?

Well, while their idea did not bear any returns immediately, they made headway in one particular area that would shape the future of their company forever.

They began to refine their ideas even more.

They spent many weeks trying to figure out just how they

would attract customers to their site and what is it that guests would like to see when they first entered the website.

These and many other questions plagued the trio as they tried, tested, and tried many ideas. Most of them rejected. Some of them just not viable.

It was during their time fine-tuning their idea that something occurred.

A revelation that was just waiting to pop out at the group.

Why do they need to target just conferences?

Why can they not work with an idea with fewer restrictions?

It was then that they realized that they could create a website where guests could book a room in someone's home. The whole process of booking would be as simple as possible. It would be as easy as booking a hotel online.

With an outburst of creative vision, they began to work on their online platform. They realized that in order for this idea to be successful, they had to ensure that the payment system that would be fluid and easy. This ensures that the customer stays on the website and does not bounce out of it. They would have to review their existing payment mechanics and create a solid website as well.

Blecharczyk was the man for the job and he immediately set his eyes up on the task.

In the meanwhile, Chesky and Gebbia were busy sourcing investors for their venture.

This would prove to be a string of disappointments and rejections for the duo.

Of all the investors that they had reached out to, most of them did not bother to respond back to them. Those that did, offered doubts about their venture.

Is the travel industry truly profitable at this point? Does their idea have a bigger scope? Were the offerings and ideas given by the founders all that there was to the project? Would the founders have a large enough market to tap into?

Among the people who responded to the three, there were those who offered their excuses for not wanting to invest their money (or even their time) in their venture.

They were unavailable at that moment and might not be able to get back to the founders in time.

They were busy with other projects.

So on, and so forth.

Chesky and Gebbia did manage to schedule a few meetings, but those would prove to be calamitous for the team as well. It was at this point that the duo's lack of experience in management and entrepreneurship would come to haunt them.

Investors were looking for the next graduate or innovator from Stanford or Harvard (think Larry Page and Sergei Brin of Google fame for Stanford and Mark Zuckerberg, the founder of Facebook, for Harvard).

Chesky and Gebbia had been part of Rhode Island School of Design (RISD.)

Many investors were turned off by the idea of renting spaces to strangers. Other found the entire concept of renting spaces weird.

But nothing came close to the experience they had with one investor in Palo Alto. They were discussing their idea with him at the University Café when, without warning, the investor simply stood up and walked out of the meeting. His half-finished drink was still on the table.

Chesky and Gebbia took a picture of the drink.

So with all of these disappointments, the duo was making no headway. It definitely seemed like the end of the road for them.

That's when Barack Obama entered the picture.

Thanks, Obama!

When Barack Obama declared his nomination for the presidency, the media were in a furor. The future president of the United States was scheduled to give his acceptance speech at the Pepsi Center in Denver, but the speech was moved to the Invesco Field. Nearly 84,000 people turned up to watch history being made.

For Chesky, Gebbia, and Blecharczyk, this was the opportunity that they had been waiting for.

They discovered that hotels in Denver would be overbooked. They need to act on the information quickly. It was probably one of the biggest opportunities that they would receive in quite a while.

Through dogged determination, they managed to get themselves included in an article on the popular online tech portal, TechCrunch. The article was written by Erick Schonfeld, and featured the title "AirBed and Breakfast Takes Pad Crashing to a Whole New Level" (you can still find the article on the web if you looked for it.)

Chesky, Gebbia, and Blecharczyk launched their site again (third time lucky? We will have to see)

The trio waited.

This time, however, they did not have to wait long. After the article got published, it started driving traffic to the website. Soon, there were enough visitors to AirBed & Breakfast to cause the site to crash. Well, the third time is not exactly the charm that they were looking for. But it did confirm something; their idea had the potential to attract customers.

What it lacked was people listing their spaces on the website.

Their problem at this point was not the demand, but the supply, which just so happened to be none at all.

Here is how was looking; people did not want to list their homes because they were not sure if anyone would book them. That created a problem for those who entered the site because they had no rooms to book.

This diffused any potential word-of-mouth marketing, which occurs when a customer uses a product and, feeling satisfied with the results, spreads the word of in his or her network of friends and acquaintances.

It was a conundrum. And they had to find a way through.

While Chesky and his colleagues may not have the management or entrepreneurial skills that are required by most founders, they did understand that a fundamental factor for any product to succeed in the market was a good marketing strategy. Most traditional or online advertisements would require a bit of investment from the trio, which they could not afford to shell out at that point.

They decided to turn their attention to another form of marketing; content. They would need to approach blogs, websites, publishers, or content creators.

Big publishers were out there looking for the big scoops. Which meant that the three founders had to reach out to smaller platforms in hopes of featuring AirBed & Breakfast on their blogs or articles.

With that decision, they reached out to as many local websites as they could discover. While we're not interested in their service, a few small blogs decided to include them in their content.

Which was all the push they needed to start a domino effect.

Using just a few small blogs, they were able to grab the attention of other smaller content creators. When these content creators featured them on their portals, bigger publishers began to take interest in the story.

Soon, the Denver Post was intent on running an article on Airbed & Breakfast. This opens up other avenues, where broadcast stations and other publishers wanted to include stories about the room sharing company.

After the launch of the stories, national media began to hone in on the trend. They were curious; who were these guys and why is this suddenly on numerous media channels?

The founders' plan was a success.

Each published story and feature brought gave them more exposure. With that exposure, their website saw listings coming through. Eventually, they had nearly 800 rooms and spaces available and almost eighty people had completed bookings.

That was the first win in their books.

They had come a long way from gaining just three booking so their website by using just three air mattresses.

At that time, Chesky, Gebbia, and Blecharczyk were using PayPal to manage the financial transactions on their website. The surge in activity created an increasing the transactions on PayPal, which eventually caused their account to be blocked on grounds of suspicious activity.

Customers who had listed their homes on the website were upset about the delay in payments. However, Chesky and Gebbia were on crowd control duty, maintaining the complaints directed towards AirBed & Breakfast. Meanwhile, Blecharczyk was on the phone with PayPal, trying to convince them to remove the restriction placed on their account.

They soon sorted out the issue, paid the customers, and got everything on track again.

Despite last-minute unexpected surprises, the team was overjoyed about the results of their work.

Their idea had worked. People were interested in listing their homes on their portal.

However, their newfound success lasted only for the duration of the convention. When the convention ended, the founders discovered traffic and listings on their site decreasing.

It was like watching a balloon deflate; people began to remove their listings in drastic numbers.

Well, third time can be the charm, but its effects may not last long.

Cereal Killers

The founders had landed back on square one.

There was no traffic on their website.

They had no more funds to spend on expensive campaigns or marketing.

More importantly, they were in debt, which was not doing them any favors under the circumstances.

They had to bounce back and they had to do it faster than one could say "AirBed & Breakfast."

Maybe not that fast, but you catch my drift.

Right now, they could not back out of the idea that they had worked on for so long. Their options would be either to change something or to add another feature into their service.

Changing something was out of the question. Not only would that take a lot of time, but they also had no idea what exactly they would have to change.

Could they add something instead? Perhaps. If they did decide to provide an addition, what exactly could that be?

Then it hit them.

The company's name was AirBed & Breakfast after all. So where was the breakfast in all of their services?

After thinking about for a while, they narrowed down their focus to cereals. Inspired from the recent convention that took place in Denver, they decided to take their cereal idea for a unique spin.

The founders created their own brand of cereals named Obama O's. To appease to the Republican side, they created another brand cheekily named Cap'n McCain's.

Initially, their idea was to get hold of a 100,000 boxes and then sell them for $2 each. That would give them enough funds as capital for the company.

Having settled on the idea (and probably convinced by the math that resulted in $200,000' worth of sales), the founders decided to enlist the help of an ex-classmate of Chesky and Gebbia's, but he was not ready to print out a 100,000 boxes for an idea that he was not confident about.

He would give them 500 boxes. He also wanted a small portion of their sale.

This created a setback for the founders. Nevertheless, Chesky and Gebbia were used to tackling difficult situations with creative thought processes.

That was when they decided that the cereal boxes would be sold as limited editions. They would print the boxes with numbers on them, market them for collectors and then sell them at $40 per box.

Now the challenge that they faced was actually getting the boxes. So instead of having to get the boxes printed, they headed to numerous supermarkets to look for the least expensive cereals that they could find.

They finally discovered cereals for a dollar per box. They bought about a thousand boxes of those cereals (the manufacturer of that cereal must definitely have been elated by that day's sale.)

They took the boxes home and began working on them. They had to flatten each box and then resealed with glue, a process that took the founders several days.

To give better exposure to their entire endeavor, the group decided to alert the media as well. There was nothing to lose and they had to give their idea every opportunity they could think of.

It was something of a surprise, but the entire idea worked instantly!

Soon, every box of Obama O's was sold out in a matter of a few days. Cap'n MacCains did not manage to sell out completely (not sure what that means though.)

And it is at this point that you are probably thinking that the founders had nailed success on the head, bagged it, and went home to create Airbnb.

If only it were that simple.

Here is what came out of their marketing stunt. They had managed to sell cereal boxes, not the idea to their website.

They did make a couple of ten thousand dollars from their cereal venture, but there was not traffic on their website. If they had decided to get into the cereal business, they might have probably made more money.

Defeated, the next few months would be a challenge for the founders, especially for two of them.

While Blecharczyk headed back to Boston to work on a new venture, Chesky and Gebbia would find themselves living on the remaining boxes of Cap'n McCain's for at least a few months (they eventually could not even afford to get the milk for the cereals.)

It was during one night in November of 2008 that Chesky and Gebbia would would into Michael Seibel again (flashback time: Seibel was the cofounder of Justin.tv that the duo had met during the design conference). During the course of the dinner, Seibel suggested that they could try to apply to Y Combinator.

Alright, time for another quick introduction into a topic. This time on Y Combinator.

Essentially, Y Combinator is a company that helps startups in their early stages of development. Commonly referred to as "seed investors" or "startup investors", they invest in companies, create connections for startups, provide mentorship, and even go so far as to pitch ideas during events and conferences.

So there you have it.

What Seibel was essentially trying to recommend was for Chesky and Gebbia to try to look for seed investment through Y Combinator.

This did not sit well with Chesky. After all, they were not in the prelaunch stages of their company. They had performed various marketing tactics. They had gotten people to list their homes on their website. They had actually earned suing their service!

The whole idea made Chesky feel like AirBed & Breakfast had not even taken off yet.

Seibel was unfazed. He even delivered a dose of the cold and harsh truth; Airbed & Breakfast was going nowhere, no matter what the founders tried. They needed investment and they needed it fast.

With a grudging acceptance of the facts, Chesky gave in to the plan. Seibel informed the two founders that the deadline for submission was over. However, he would get in touch with Paul Graham, founder of Y Combinator, to see if there was spot for one more entry.

Seibel got a message out to Paul Graham, who claimed he would take them on if they submitted the application by midnight. The duo applied and received an interview date. At this point, they had to convince Blecharczyk to return to San Francisco and succeeded in doing it.

One of the things to note at this point is that the application process for Y Combinator can be quite taxing. The interviews were only rumored to last for ten minutes and they consisted of Graham and his partners asking questions in rapid fire succession for five minutes. There was no allowance for presentations.

After a few hours of preparations, both Brian and Chesky were ready for it. On the way out, Gebbia tried to grab one of the cereal boxes that they had sold earlier and put it in his bag, but the other partners stopped him. It was as if they were telling him that the time for gimmicks had passed (Gebbia still managed to somehow take a few boxes and stuff them in a bad). They drove to Mountain View to the headquarters of Y Combinator.

And here was where the real test began.

The interview was a grueling process. Graham was not entirely happy with the idea of AirBed & Breakfast. He was impressed with Chesky's and Gebbia's knowledge of the market (after all, they did spend a considerable time marketing their product), but he was clearly not sold on their idea. Things were looking grim for the founders of AirBed & Breakfast.

The interview had finally come to an end. No progress was made and it just seemed like they had drawn the last straw.

In a last-ditch effort, Gebbia pulled out the cereal boxes (the Obama O's and Cap'n McCain's) that he had snuck into his bag. He then took them to Graham, who at the time was talking to his partners, and handed him one of them. The entire gesture was rather odd (you would be surprised too if someone handed you a cereal box at the end of an interview). Graham had no response to give except thank Gebbia, thinking that the box was a gesture of courtesy. The founders then revealed they had actually made and then resold the boxes in order to fund their enterprise. That caught Graham's attention. Astounded by their creativity to adapt to their situation despite what he believed was an insane idea.

Gebbia's stunt would be the move that would give Graham some encouragement to think about the idea of the founders.

They needed to be on standby should they be accepted so that they could be ready to move immediately - otherwise, the slot would go on to the next person.

This is it right? This is the moment they have been waiting for. I believe those might be the thoughts going through your head right now.

Well, no.

On the way, Chesky got a call from Graham. He answered the call and with Gebbia and Blecharczyk listening in, spoke to Graham. Just as Graham was about to reveal something important, the call disconnected.

A worst time for a poor connection, if there ever was one in the lives of the three founders.

The trio returned back to San Francisco, dejected and of course, feeling unlucky.

It was then that they received a call from Graham again.

And that right there was the moment they have been waiting for.

Paul Graham had finally accepted to provide funding for the trio's venture. He would invest $20,000. He would have 6% stake in the company.

He would also give them three months to come up with something.

That is what the founders had.

Three months.

New York, New York

It was time for an intervention.

Paul Graham sat down with the three founders and asked questions about their company. Most particularly, he wanted to know details about their customers (those who listed their homes on their site). After all, there is much to learn from the users, since they are the ones using the system.

When asked where most of their users were located, Chesky, Gebbia, and Blecharczyk responded that they were in New York.

Graham immediately suggested that New York is where they should go. They needed to interact with their users and find out where the faults lie in the system.

While Blecharczyk stayed back to code on the system, Chesky and Gebbia headed over to New York to find out more about their user base.

Once in New York, the two founders had to literally knock on doors and stay at the homes of their users. They wanted to know how the homes were displayed online and what tactics were used to attract guests.

What they discovered was that the images used to list the homes were not that great. It did not matter if the service was impeccable of if the users maintained their homes well in real life, the photos did not do justice to the service or the space.

They had to find a way to capture incredible photos of the homes.

Problem is, neither Chesky nor Gebbia had enough funds to even purchase a decent camera.

And so, they got in touch with a friend (someone who was their classmate at Rhode Island School of Design) and borrowed a DSLR from him.

Using that camera, they went to each and every house and took pictures for their users.

Yup, they became photographers overnight, making certain that the listings on their website looked as good as the homes themselves.

After using the high-quality images online, they immediately began to notice the change in guests' responses on the site. More and more users began to book rooms using their site.

Using this tactic, they began to focus on other cities as well.

When they received a decent return from the changes they made to their listings, they began to hire photographers to work on listings in other cities.

That simple idea led to more growth.

Moreover, Chesky and Gebbia began to take user and guest feedback. Gebbia in fact used his own mobile phone to answer more of the queries that came to the group. They would communicate any valuable feedback to Blecharczyk, who would then work on the changes required for the website.

In such small ways, they were able to improve the website even more, making it easier for anyone to use the website.

However, it was not until a musician posed them a request that changed the way they began to look at Airbed & Breakfast.

He asked them if he could rent out his entire apartment while he was away on a tour. The founders immediately refused the request.

But the more they thought about the idea, the more they realized that it made a lot of sense. They could open up more potential for them to explore and more opportunities for the business to grow.

Initially, they had made it mandatory for the users to provide the guests with breakfast. After their conversation with the musician, they decided to remove the breakfast condition and instead provide an option to rent out the entire apartment to guests.

This means that the name AirBed & Breakfast would not be a matching name for their company, as it spoke of the inclusion of breakfast in all their listings.

They decided to change that.

Their first idea was to shorten the name to "Airbanb."

When they thought about the name a little more, they discovered that it oddly sounded similar to "Airband."

Hence, they shortened the name even further.

And that my friends, was how "Airbnb" was formed.

Chapter 3: After Initial Revenue

The initial revenue was not much.

Before we talk about that, let us focus on what the team had achieved.

Y Combinator used to schedule an event called "Demo Day". This was where startups could present their ideas and seek finance and initial capital from investors. Chesky and the team had a big opportunity ahead of them. They needed to make a big impression.

During the 2009 Demo day, the team explained their idea to the crowd.

This time however, they were not struck by bad fortune.

In fact, Greg McAdoo, representing Sequoia Capital provided $600,000 in seed investment for Airbnb.

Time for lesson number three.

You are probably wondering what Sequoia Capital is. Let me explain. In simple terms, it is a venture capital firm. These firms seek out businesses in their early stages or emerging ideas that need funding and invest in them. They evaluate the potential of the venture, and if they find that the entire business endeavor is profitable, then they provide an initial boost to the venture through a seed investment.

That means that Airbnb successfully managed to raise a good amount to get started. The founders were thrilled. In fact, they never expected anyone to consider investing in their idea (probably due to the many disappointments provided by previous investors).

Receiving the confidence of someone was a big step for them.

The three founders had finally succeeded.

After much trials and tribulations (not to mention a few months' worth of Cap'n McCains), they had the foundations to start focusing on their company.

What next?

Well, like any other company, they needed to pay attention to the bigger picture. They need to create a long-term strategy. They needed a company vision and mission. As soon as their thoughts drifted to the idea of managing their company, they realized another important factor to run a successful company; employees.

The need to add more people to the team had its own challenges. Having worked eighteen hours a day for seven days a week, they needed to find people who would show a sense of passion and commitment towards the company.

In short, they needed to hire the right people. That is easier said than done right?

What they were looking for was not to hire someone who would add new features to the platform. They could do that. Eventually.

They needed someone who would share the vision of the company and, in turn, attract many more like him or her.

In order to attract the right talent towards the company, they had to form a culture.

An office culture is often overlooked. Many are of the opinion that as long as you have the people doing the job, you simply had to focus on getting more output from those people.

However, that is a short-term strategy. Hoping that a mere push for the employees will guarantee any positive results is purely a hypothetical scenario. An office culture allows each employee to get a 'feel' for the company. If they like what they see, then they might stay longer in the company.

Chesky and Gebbia understood this basic fact. All they needed was to find out what kind of culture they would like to adopt within Airbnb.

They looked to other companies for inspiration. In fact, they went as far as to reach out to companies to find out more about their culture. Their list was nothing short of impressive.

Starbucks, Nike, Apple, Zappos and many others were part of their list.

But it was Zappos, the shoe manufacturer, which truly attracted their attention. There was something about the friendly and unconventional atmosphere at Zappos that Chesky and Gebbia wanted to replicate in Airbnb.

This meant that they needed to know more about Zappos' work culture. In order to do so, they got in touch with the CEO of the company, Tony Hsieh. Within days, they were touring Zappos' headquarters, getting valuable pointers form the CEO himself.

After their tour, they got together to find out just what they had learned, not just from the shoe and clothing retailer whose headquarters they had looked at, but also form the other companies they were taking inspiration from.

What was the secret process that enabled these companies to work the way they did?

The answer was plain and simple: each of the companies had

a set of vision and mission statements – or "core values" in other words – that not only guided the business organization's internal work processes, but also enveloped their goals and targets.

It defined how the company would move forward and what they wanted to achieve in the long run. Core values determined how a company would interact with the customers, shareholders, suppliers, and other groups of people that it came into contact with.

This led Chesky, Gebbia, and Blecharczyk to form their own core values for Airbnb. While the company had numerous changes made to their core values, some of them remained even to this day. Here are four of their most essential values:

- Champion the mission

Chesky knew what it took and his fellow co-founders to reach where they were. They were looking for the same zeal and ambition in their employees.

There would be no compromise in that department.

- Be a host

The three founders wanted to bring in people who would value the hospitality industry, understand its propensity to be profitable and know, without doubt, that the company can succeed in the industry despite any odd.

- Every frame matters

Every detail matters. As Chesky and Gebbia had themselves experienced when they were looking at homes and taking better pictures for their website, they knew that no detail should go overlooked.

- Embrace the adventure

They wanted their employees to learn. There should a thirst for new ideas and knowledge that should not diminish easily. If they were going to involve people in their company, those people should be curious about new things.

With those values firmly established, it was time to bring in the manpower.

After finalizing the core values, they set down to interview the candidates. This was no easy process. They had to go through multiple candidates. They spent not just days getting to know each candidate, but months.

The process was long and arduous, but the three founders were of the belief that if they had to get something right, might as well get in right in the first try.

This notion of making the best pick for the first employee eventually led to them to Nick Grandy.

Here is something you should know about Grandy. He had started his own company named Wundrbar. However, his search-oriented company had not taken off successfully. He had also been part of Y Cobinator, hoping to discover some sort of success in nailing down an investor for this failed business.

After meeting Chesky and Gebbia, he began to believe in the entire concept of Airbnb. He knew that as a creator himself, he could offer more to the company in terms of its growth, innovations, and product. He saw how people used the platform and wanted that to translate into a product that could gain massive appeal.

Chesky and Gabbia knew they had their man.

All that was required was to get Grandy on board and get him started on his role.

What followed was a series of interviews to test Grandy's mettle and truly decide if he was the person they had been looking for. Eventually, all founders were satisfied with their pick and Grandy started working for Airbnb as an engineer.

Soon after, their team began to grow. At first, they focused on hiring more engineers. They need the team of tech specialists to refine the platform to its most polished state. Once there were enough engineers in the team, the founders then decided to bring in customer service representatives.

Here is a fact for you to know; the interview process was intense. One of the engineers hired for the job (who would later go on to become the Vice President of product), clearly remembers that the entire interview – if it could be condensed into an hourly period – was nearly fifteen hours long. Of course, the whole process took place over several months, during multiple meetings and discussions, phone calls, and tests.

I almost skipped a part. The engineer's name is Joe Zadeh.

One of the things that drew Zedeh to Airbnb was the excitement that he noticed among all the employees at Airbnb. That and his interview with Chesky and Gebbia (apparently they had talked about superpowers).

Zadeh was impressed. He knew that he was going to part of something big and he wanted to start as soon as possible.

With that, that, Airbnb had a team.

Growth Phase

Now at that time Airbnb was still an unknown brand. While there were new listings on the platform, the traction gained was slow that awareness about the platform was not spreading as fast as the founders would have liked.

They needed to boost the awareness of the company more.

The company was attracting listings on its platform solely through word-of-mouth marketing. That marketing process seemed to generate new leads and customers at a snail's pace.

It was Blecharczyk – always using his tech knowledge – who recommended using two platforms to generate a massive increase in their reach; Google and Craigslist.

On Google, Blecharczyk utilized the power of Google AdWords. He fine-tuned Google ads to reach out to people in different locations. Each ad would be customized based on the city they would target. This allowed the founders to add a personal touch to their promotional activities.

Craigslist had a massive reach in 2009. It boasted more than tens of millions of members on its platform and this allowed the perfect opportunity for several businesses and entrepreneurs to market their products.

Using a clever algorithm, Blecharczyk allowed users on Airbnb to post their listings instantly on Craigslist. This provided benefits to both the users and to Airbnb.

Users could now reach out to more people. The potential to get the people interested in their homes and spaces magnified tremendously. After all, you now had two platforms showcasing the offerings on Airbnb.

For Airbnb, that meant that their listings would receive faster responses from potential guests and the chance for more Craigslist users to see the advertisements posted by Airbnb hosts. This would encourage more people to become hosts themselves and in turn, would create a bigger market for guests.

It was a smart plan and it helped the company reach newer heights.

However, it was still not enough to give the company the momentum that it needed.

Let's take a look at how Airbnb functions.

The first thing to remember is that hosting a home, space, apartment or any other form of lodging is free on Airbnb. Gusts can also come over to the platform and look at the listings for free.

So where does the company make its revenue?

That happens through a commission structure.

Every time a host receives a booking, Airbnb takes about 3% commission from the host. That does not sound like it could get the company to the billion-dollar status that it enjoys today. There should be something else, you might think.

Well, you are right.

Airbnb also takes a 6-12% commission from the guests as well. This allowed them to act as an intermediary with the only difference being that they will not interfere with the transactions between host and guest, unless necessary or in the event of a crisis.

One of the features used by Airbnb is that the company holds the funds for a 24-hour period before releasing it to the host. This is to ensure that after the traveler checks into a room or a space, he or she is satisfied with what they find. In the unlikely event that a host has tricked a guest with false images of the lodging, the guest can cancel the transaction and the host receives no payment from Airbnb.

With this, Airbnb started receiving feedback on their rooms. Editors, journalists, and anyone else who wanted to experience Airbnb were all ready to head out and live in one of the rooms listed on their website. They wanted to know what it felt like to live in a stranger's home. And after that, give their reviews on the website.

Jessica Salter, a writer from the Telegraph (which is an online newspaper), narrated her experience with Airbnb in 2012 when she visited San Francisco. Her host was 'Jason,' who was not within the vicinity at the time and had left her the keys to the apartment. He also left a note saying that there were bagels in the freezer and snacks in the cupboard. The host also gave details concerning where to get coffee in the area, the Wifi login details, and even the Netflix account details should she get bored. She recounted that it was a bit strange to see the evidence of another person's life. She could see signs of his girlfriend considering the couple's photos were all around (there were even wedding invitations on the fridge). Her review of the experience was positive.

A Matter of Trust

Airbnb is a marketplace for rooms and lodgings. It really is as simple as that. But what makes it effective is how it handles its users and its monetization process.

As a marketplace, it works on two sides. You have the hosts, who can list their homes free and get charged for every booking made on their listings.

On the other hand, you have the travelers whom Airbnb monetizes for every booking that they make on the portal

So far, we have understood that essential part.

On a platform such as Airbnb, there is an imbalance between the listings and the bookings. You see, there are more travelers looking for places to bunk than there are home stays, rooms, and spaces available for them. This means that Airbnb is a marketplace where the demand is much higher than the supply.

Now in typical circumstances, a business would always focuses on creating a balance between the supply and the demand. This is because if demand increase and eventually overtakes the supply rate, then there tends to be a surplus of need for the product. This means that the only way to curb that demand would be to increase the prices of the products. Airbnb cannot increase room rates. This would defeat the purpose of the website and might cause people to turn away from the application.

On the other hand, they cannot keep the demand higher at all times. This might cause disappointments among the customers seeking to find rooms for rent. Eventually, fewer people might come to rely on the platform.

Is should be noted that it is far easier to work on increasing the customers to the platform. They simply have to showcase some of the homes they provide (which are fascinating and in many cases, quite inviting). The trick is to increase the number of people who would like to set up their homes for rent. Not everyone is comfortable with the idea of letting strangers reside within their homes for any length of time.

This is why, Airbnb provides more benefits to the hosts than the guests. You might wonder why that is. Before I answer that, let us look at what benefits hosts receive and why it is essential to pay attention to them.

Anyone listing their homes on the website have to provide only 3% of the booking fee. Airbnb also provides them with free professional photography services (available in many countries and spreading to every country where Airbnb is present). Apart from this, they invite top hosts to events and parties, mail gifts and other decorative items to the hosts, and more.

All of this is done in order to allow the hosts to enjoy a comfortable experience using the app. They also want this to influence the hosts to use word-of-mouth form of marketing to encourage other people to become hosts.

In the end, it is similar to a domino effect. You take care of the hosts, who then spread good word about your platform to others, who, in turn, begin to list their homes on the platform.

On the travelers' side, they begin to see more options to book spaces. More users begin to use the platform, noticing the growing number of available rooms. Additionally, more homes also mean that the growing demand on the platform is being satisfied. This eventually shows potential hosts that there is an increasing customer base on Airbnb, which creates more listings, and the story goes on.

By simply focusing on one essential aspect on their platform, Chesk, Gebbia, and Blecharczyk were able to capitalize on an effective form of marketing.

Another benefit to their strategy of focusing on the hosts is this: if more hosts increase and more guests begin to the book on the platform, those guests can become hosts themselves.

Let us assume this scenario.

A traveler from Singapore flies to London. He books a room through Airbnb and eventually makes his way to the host's place. He is impressed with the room he was staying in and the way the host was earning money using Airbnb. Once the traveler returns home to his country, he decides to become a host himself.

That way, a host is created in Singapore.

When residents of Singapore notice that there is an Airbnb host in their country, they might wonder if they could become hosts themselves. Not every individual might convert into an Airbnb host, but it only takes a few to spread the word of the platform even more.

That creates a chain reaction. With more people becoming aware of making a quick buck on an app, more listings appear on the platform. Eventually, you might have someone from Thailand visiting Singapore and wondering if he or she could become a host back in his or her home country.

This is why Airbnb pays more interest to the situation of their hosts.

However, that did not mean that they were ignorant of the needs of the guests or considered them inessential for marketing purposes.

Trust was an essential factor on the platform. Despite how effectively they were able to market Airbnb to different countries of the world, it still boiled down to the trust between the parties involved in the transaction (which would be the hosts and the guests).

For Airbnb to work in the market, people had to come to terms with the idea that the hosts they were about to meet could be trustworthy. This was no easy impression to make in the minds of the users. Guests book online, but the experiences they have are offline and within the physical world. That meant that Airbnb had to facilitate the right digital tools that would enable guests to have some form of face-to-face interaction with the hosts or discover some useful feedback about the hosts. This brought them to the below factors:

- User profiles of the hosts
- Reviews and rating criteria

The founders came to learn that for trust purposes, allowing the person who was responsible for the listing to upload a real picture of himself or herself made quite a big difference. Guests were able to humanize the entire experience, giving them the confident that there was a real person who was being the listings.

This may sound rather odd. But think of it this way: you came across a guest profile on Airbnb with the username "Guestboy123" and the profile image of an alligator, I am not sure if you would feel comfortable staying at that person's place. Who knows what Guestboy 123 the alligator is hiding in his home?

This feature of adding a profile picture made Airbnb have a human element in the same way that Facebook and other social networks provide to their users. In fact, there are numerous blogs and articles on how to gain the trust of potential guests by using the right profile picture!

Now let us look at the second factor to improve trust on the platform.

By providing people the ability to rate and review the places and rooms of hosts, they help other become aware of their experiences. This allows future guests to avoid hosts that do not provide satisfactory services, may have malicious intent, have used false advertisements, or are even neglectful of the guests that stay within their premises. This has two vital impact on the Airbnb experience:

- Hosts who utilize duplicitous methods to list their homes, provide subpar services, or are even capable of causing harm to the guests immediately find themselves with fewer guests. This way, the platform is able to remove those services that do not meet the Airbnb standards.

- Hosts are able to build more trust. The remaining hosts who provide the right services, experience, and treatment to the guests are those that help raise the trust of the platform in the eyes of the costumer.

When the Going Gets Tough

While Airbnb did place strict measures to improve trust among its users, there were incidents that gave the public cause for concern. Probably even outrage.

One such incident occurred in 2011, less than a week after the company had announced the funding for series B in 2011.

The story involves a host and damaged property.

Yes, you might probably have guessed where this tale is heading.

A certain host on the platform got home after a month long excursion only to find that her home has been completely razed by the guests she was hosting. They had smashed a hole through the closet door and found passports, cash, credit cards, and jewellery hidden inside the closet. They even took her things - a camera, laptop, iPod, and external backup drives.

This of course, did not sit well with the host.

I mean, what would you do if you returned home to find everything that is valuable to you is now in the hands of someone who is probably halfway across the globe?

After Airbnb conducted their investigation, they discovered that the guest had used a falsified ID and a stolen credit card to make the booking. This revealed a flaw in the booking system that allows users to skip the identification verification process up on payment. To make matters worse, it was up to the host platform, Airbnb, to respond to the issue.

Which they did, sort of.

You see, the host later claimed that one of the founders had contacted her. She went on to say that the founder had requested her to tone down the damages she claimed were done to her property.

Obviously, this situation was all the fuel the media needed to stoke the anti-Airbnb fire. The situation turned into a media storm and there was a public outcry especially considering that fact that the situation confirmed the beliefs of many people; those who knew that the platform would harm to the guests and hosts.

Eventually, Chesky provided a public apology and mentioned that the company had messed up by not implementing proper checks and balances beforehand.

The company then came up with a $50,000 guarantee, which they placed to protect the hosts from damage by their guests. They even set up a 24-hour customer hotline and a Safety and Trust department, both of which were responsible for crisis management and responding to hosts as soon as possible.

Problems to hosts and unwanted media attention were not the only problems that Airbnb had to face.

Suddenly any chateau, villa, or even two bedroom apartments could become the getaway of choice for holiday goers. This made revenue increase for independent homeowners and other residents, provided they had the means to list their homes on Airbnb. The governments and other locals did not like the developments one bit, though. They blamed Airbnb and the hosts of other short-term rental companies for pricing out long-term renting residents and side stepping the regulations that are usually placed on the hotel industry and registered apartments.

Considering Airbnb is a global phenomenon, the United States was not the only country where the issue of allow guests to rent out private properties without regulations came into play.

The latest country to introduce strict regulations on the matter of Airbnb listings was Japan. Recently, the platform had to remove several thousands of listings and even cancel reservations because of a new law enacted by the government to highlight just what private residences could do. Airbnb was in outcry regarding the incident and claimed it was contrary to the guidance provided by the Japanese Tourism Agency to the Airbnb team. The company noted that the new rules affected the travel experiences of several thousands of visitors to the nation.

According to the regulations, anyone who wanted to list properties on the site would have to register their accommodations with the local government. Then Japanese government impressedup on the notion that this regulation could provide the local government the ability to conduct safety checks on the listed homes.

The regulations also set limits on the listings. The time that one could rent their property to travelers was restricted to 180 days every year, and there were very hefty fines for those found in non-compliance to the new regulations.

Then other countries and cities began to place their restrictions.

In 2017, the city of Amsterdam had 2.5 million overnight stays.

These were the stays that occurred solely through Airbnb. In 2018, city officials announced some very radical measures that were meant to ban the short-term rental systems brought by Airbnb and their counterparts in the busy areas. The goal of this exercise allegedly was to reduce overall tourism.

Palma de Mallorca was the first Spanish city that initiated a ban on renting apartments to tourists regardless of the platform used to make those rentals. The city's focus was a crackdown on companies like Airbnb, which the local residents claimed were increasing the rates of rent.

Barcelona is currently involved in a legal dispute with the firm. The city council fined the booking company €600,000 ($677,082) in 2016 for marketing flats that did not have a license. In a bid to control the rise of such flats, city officials sent out inspectors in a citywide hunt to find hosts who did not have the right paperwork for renting their apartments, houses, or rooms.

It seemed as though things were getting challenging for the company, especially considering the fact that they depended on countries around the world supporting their venture.

After all, without allowing travelers to find places to stay in other countries what else could they market?

Soon, the hotel industry decided to provide opposition too (this was bound to happen eventually as they were disrupting the hotel industry).

Airbnb makes it easier to find better - and sometimes cheaper - accommodation within some of the most desired areas. In this way, they undercut the prices charged by the bed and breakfasts and the hotels. The Economist periodical claimed three years ago that if the firm continues its current growth, it would be taking a 10% bite from the bottom line of hotels, which is sufficient to make a dent in any industry.

At first, hotel executives were not eager to admit the effect Airbnb had on their revenue drops. This is probably because they were experiencing significant booms since 2008, a time when industries were feeling the economic heat.

You see, the hotel industry has generally two responses to the rise in short-term rentals; these responses would be either denial or panic. The ones in denial have the idea that Airbnb and similar types of businesses serve a different type of market. According to the hotels, the customer profile that goes for Airbnb is someone that prefers the local cuisine and wants to immerse himself or herself in the experience, which the traveler can attain by renting an extra room in an apartment.

However, hotels soon realized that there was another way that Airbnb could threaten their industry.

Alright, time for another primer on how some hotels work and make profits.

When it is peak tourist season, most hotels are completely booked by traveler. Some traveler even place advance booking on the hotels in order to get the best rooms possible or jump ahead of the crowd.

When this happens, there is a shortage of hotel rooms. This allows hotels to increase their prices. In fact, some hotels have known to double - and even triple - their rates during tourist season.

Essentially, this happens because of the shortage. In other words, the when the demand far outweighs the supply, hotel room rates skyrocket.

But what happens when tourists can find a cheaper alternative?

What if there was a company like Airbnb that offered travelers the chance to find not just suitable accommodations, but more features than what they could find in a hotel? This, combined with the fact that these travelers can truly enjoy a local experience on their holiday, led to more bookings done on Airbnb.

With increased bookings, Airbnb began to market itself automatically to other travelers, leading to even more bookings (and of course, more listings as well).

You now have apartments, houses, and other lodgings practically replacing hotel rooms.

This means that the demand that allowed hotel rooms to increase their rates was not there anymore.

This also means that hotels had to lower their rates in order to attract more customers.

Not a good situation for hotels to encounter. Which means that they would have to oppose the entity that created this shortage of demand.

Furthermore, to make matters worse, hosts on Airbnb could control the prices of their rooms as well. This resulted in a situation where they could enjoy the profits that otherwise the hotels would be enjoying.

Enter the Lobbyists

In a presentation in 2016, the American Lodging Association, which is a trade group that holds the Hilton Worldwide, Hyatt, and Marriott International Hotels, praised an investigation into the way Airbnb affects housing costs. This was part of an unconventional plan to further opposition against Airbnb. The plan included a multifaceted campaign at the state, local, and federal levels.

At this point, it seemed that hotels were not taking any chances with Airbnb.

However, the association went on to admit the push against Airbnb was not about the financial effect they have had on the hotel industry. Troy Flanagan, Vice President of the American Hotel and Lodging Association, maintains that Airbnb is a lodging industry that does not seem to be playing by the same rules as the others who are operating in the same field. There were also other initiatives by the association, some of them included plans to get the state attorneys and local politicians to hamper the level of eligible hosts in their jurisdictions. What that means is that they wanted government officials to restrict the number of hosts in the city. That would definitely affect Airbnb's business model as they rely on gathering more hosts in the country or city that they operate within.

The association also began funding studies that illustrate the fact that Airbnb has many hosts who seem to be running "hotels" from their residential complexes with full knowledge of their actions. They were also of the opinion that these hosts were showing open negligence for what they are doing. The studies were also aiming to highlight how Airbnb hosts do not collect the hotel taxes as the hotel industry does, and they are not subject to the same rules on safety.

In the target markets such as New York, the hotel industry began to source the local affiliates working with the office of the Governor and the state legislator in order to help implement steeper level fines for the hosts that list on Airbnb.

It seemed that for every success that Airbnb faced, there were a multitude of challenges that awaited them.

The Art of Being Popular

You have to realize that there were other entities that provided peer-to-peer short-term rental services.

You had companies like Couchsurfing and HomeAway giving similar options as that of Airbnb to the masses. Even Craigslist had a special section for people to place ads about place they would like to rent out.

So why did they succeed while all the other brands did not? Okay, perhaps the other brands succeeded as well to a certain degree.

What I meant was this: why couldn't the other entities manage to attain the level of success and popularity that Airbnb did?

In order to answer this question, we need to look at the very service that Airbnb is offering. Actually, to be more precise, it is the platform on which the services are provided that makes a difference.

It is the aesthetics of Airbnb's website and the app. It is the way you can book rooms on the platform. It is the convenience that you receive every time you enter the website or app.

All of these and more contribute to the success of Airbnb in the market.

Another contributor could be the presence of the sharing economy. The development of the sharing economy is what primed the market to get ready for Airbnb, though the founders did not know it at the time. People had been sharing all manner of services; however, no one had yet come with the option of staying at someone else's home in order to gain a local experience.

If you wondering what sharing services I am talking about, then you only need to look at a few examples.

You had talent sharing platforms such as Upwork, ride sharing applications and services like Uber and Lyft and knowledge sharing sources such as Quora.

Each one had gotten the public used to sharing knowledge, skills, and services with others.

So when Airbnb entered the scene, the timing was perfect. When other apps that are similar to Airbnb arrived in the short-term rental sphere earlier, they did not enjoy the opportunity presented by sharing services the way Airbnb did.

Furthermore, the founders had a design background. This might have turned investors away from their project, but it definitely contributed to the overall feel of Airbnb. Chesky and Gebbia were pedantic about their company. They would look at everything to make sure it worked and felt right. The design of the app had to be perfect. The user journey had to be simple and fluid. Even the manner in which the search function worked had to meet the standards set by the founders.

The entire website was composed of many elements (just like any other service providing online portal).

You had the payment mechanisms, the customer service capabilities, and even the review features. While these elements are not special, it is the way that they were integrated together that made Airbnb different from the rest of the companies providing the same service.

Among all of the aforementioned elements, the payment system was the most complex. When they realized that it took the user too many steps to make a specific payment, they decided to scrap the mechanisms they already had in place and build a new one from scratch.

This is what led the team to become the intermediary. They would hold on to the money for a temporary period of time (currently 24-hours) and then remit the money to the hosts once the transaction had been deemed satisfactory.

This mechanism was one that was not present in other companies. No had come up with the idea to protect the user experience in the manner that Airbnb was doing (and still continue to do so).

Of course, not everything was down to luck.

As you have read until now, a lot of the work that had gone into making the company was pure determination, strategy, and persistence.

Weighing the Scales

Through all the challenges that the company faced, they were beginning to scale. Every experience that they had faced before was a lesson for them to learn. They understood their mistakes and were willing to perform remedial actions to settle complicated matters. They knew that they were still not perfect, but they were willing to learn and grow nevertheless.

This is why, despite the odds stacked against them they found that users were confident about Airbnb.

Back when they had started with the idea of Airbnb (or rather "Airbed & Breakfast"), the whole idea was to simply survive. They had to make sure that their company did not crumble under the immense pressure that they were facing.

After all, when a company is on the verge of losing everything, not many people think about the next 5-year plan.

Now, Airbnb was in a new playing field. Their challenges are more complex. Creating bed paces for conference attendees and living on cereal boxes might have seemed difficult, but they were rather straightforward challenges. You had a problem and you just had to find a solution to the problem any way you could.

But today, every problem might have multiple solutions and all of those solutions could seem the right thing to do.

However, one wrong move and their entire reputation would be in jeopardy. They have to face competitions. They have to tackle crisis that could send the wrong information to the public and even create a media frenzy (remember the host whose property got damaged?)

They even have to face the governments of countries.

I say, give me a cereal box any day.

By late 2011, the company had managed to bring in 150 employees and add more in their overseas branches. It was not a massive increase when you think about it but it is a spectacular growth when you realize that Airbnb was officially launched in 2008.

The company was definitely scaling.

There were millions of users on the platform but not enough customer service agents to represent them. They were not growing fast enough. At least, their team wasn't scaling to meet the growing customer base on their platform.

Chesky, Gebbia, and Blecharczyk kept the growth going, managing to tackle any situation that came their way with deftness and experience.

In 2012, Chesky was getting a feel for the company's momentum. He understood that they could not slow down and so he made sure that the users on the platform were taken care of.

Soon, the founders made a move to bigger headquarters. It was the year 2013.

It had gone from becoming just another story in Silicon Valley to a model for other businesses. Any company based on the sharing economy would often classify themselves as the "Airbnb" of a certain business.

Chapter 4: And In Recent Beginnings

The founding of Airbnb and its growth to become the entity it is now is a story that is nothing short of exemplary.

Everything - from the challenges and struggles that the founders faced even before they launched the company to the opposition bombarding the company from many corners – highlights the tremendous nature of determination against unbelievable odds. It is Hercules versus Hydra saga, where Hercules is a technological company and the Hydra's many heads are the many problems that the company had to face during its life. What is surprising to note is that the founders raised the company within a few years. They had no prior entrepreneurial and business experience.

In fact, two of them were design students; not exactly the kind of skills you might look for in founders.

Today, the company employs close to 2,500 people in its offices. When you get into the Airbnb office in San Francisco, the first impression you make is that the office is a trendy type of apartment that you can find anywhere in the world. This design is aligned with the theme of one of the company's objective: to create a world where a person could belong in any environment. It is pertinent that the home sharing corporate headquarters is styled in a manner that is inviting to just about anyone in the society.

However, to simply look at the company and its office setting is forgetting its true strength.

Airbnb is not merely the employees it holds with the walls of its headquarters. It is the millions of hosts around the world who get to turn their homes into rental spaces. It is the millions of guests who get to become a part of the Airbnb experience.

In the beginning, Airbnb was simply a model for cheap rental spaces. People who could not afford to rent out hotel rooms would look to Airbnb for answers. Eventually, the brand became a tool that many millennials would use to find a space for a temporary stay. As the company grew even more, it was not only to represent the inexpensive rental spaces around the world; it was a platform to find a truly unique service. It was a portal to discover experiences one cannot find anywhere else.

In fact, Gwyneth Paltrow had spent close to $8,000 to spend in an Airbnb listing.

It was not all about inexpensive listings. It was about offering something no other hotel or room rentals in the world could offer.

The idea of Gwyneth Paltrow making a booking through Airbnb showed something:

- It had become a tool to highlight some of the most sophisticated, exemplary, and unique room spaces for travelers.
- It had turned into a platform that was accessible to anyone, regardless of their income status.

You could decide to spend less on Airbnb and you would still find many options that would meet your tastes and preferences. Or alternatively, could be one of the people who enjoys splurging on getting things and you will have something waiting for you on Airbnb.

One of the things that you can notice when you are using the platform is the type of properties scattered across the globe. You could spend less than $20 to stay in a guest house in Bali with an attached swimming pool or you could shell out more than a $1,000 to enjoy a fully furnished apartment in Paris. In fact, even within a specific city, you could discover with various price tags. With less than $30, you could be staying in a room with a king-sized bed in New York. However, if you wish, you could spend more than $2,000 and find yourself in luxury accommodations. The choice is all yours.

Because of the many options that were cropping up on Airbnb, a trend was slowly starting to emerge. This trend was related to the way people were looking at rental spaces around the world.

The demand for peer-to-peer types of accommodation such as Airbnb began growing at a faster rate than that of conventional leisure locations such as hotels and resorts. There are, of course, direct economic effects to the bottom lines of both customer and host considering the lower price levels compared to that of resorts at the same locations. However, there are also the trendiness and "cool" factors that spawned from using such platforms. This increases the potential for the customer to opt for something unique when selecting holiday destinations.

Because of the demand for services like Airbnb, you now have other companies who are trying to replicate the success made by the rental hosting company founded by Chesky, Gebbia, and Blecharczyk.

Just perform a quick Google search and you will find options like Booking.com, Homestay, OneFineStay and VillasDirect.

Everyone seemed eager to jump in on the holiday rental market. Why wouldn't they? The potential was huge and turning into a billion dollar company was definitely tempting.

When the Price is Nice

With all the news about hotel chains making a move against Airbnb, won't that actually affect the business of the company? Won't that affect demand?

Not quite. At least, nothing might happen in the present or near future.

There are many reasons that make Airbnb the brand it is today. You do not reach a certain level by simply focusing on one aspect and hoping that it works well for you.

One of the essential factors that makes Airbnb favorable (and even preferable) by many users is the price. Hotel chains are restricted to stay within a certain price bracket. A hotel that offers you a room for $800a night cannot simply bring down that price to $100a night. However, with Airbnb, you can find two similar forms of accommodations for surprisingly different price tags. It definitely goes to show the diversity that the platform offers to the users.

Another reason for Airbnb's success is something that is not frequently mentioned, but is still a vital part of the company's growth.

Airbnb understood the dissatisfaction that users felt about big hotels. The better way to explain this dissatisfaction is through an example. Let us assume that you have decided to spend your holiday in Thailand. You decide to book a hotel in the country for your stay. This particular hotel is extremely modern and comes with some spectacular designs.

However, you are there to experience Thailand. You definitely do not want to feel like you are in a hotel in New York. Sure, the hotel you are staying in provides some luxurious features, but they take away the spirit of the holiday.

In a similar manner, people want to wake up in their holidays feeling like that have experienced the land they have visited and its culture.

This is particularly true for millennial travelers. Providing these travelers with exemplary breakfast options with the most delicious Crème brûlée in the world might sound like a selling point for many hotels, but they do not fit the culture of a country like Vietnam or Spain.

These days, travelers want to create custom experiences. They want to show others that they have blended into the culture and atmosphere of the locals in the country they visit. They want to feel the authenticity of the place they are visiting.

Airbnb gives travelers that option. It helps them create a different and unique experience that they would love to share with others.

Additionally, Airbnb gives the travelers the option to stay out of the main roads. Most hotels would not typically think of locating themselves in remote, off-beaten areas. However, just give a quick flick on Airbnb and you will be shown a list of spaces that are not embedded within the busy (and often loud and disruptive), tourist spots of the city.

This is a magnet that Airbnb uses to attract new customers and it is frankly one that hotels cannot boast about.

Previously, you could find such unique listings on local classifieds or if through connections you made in the country you are travelling to. With Airbnb, you skip the lengthy process of researching such unique places because everything is already listed for you within a specific platform.

I can give you an example of this. I enjoy staying at the next luxury hotel as much as anyone else. However, recently, I have discovered a tendency to skip hotels altogether. The number of incredible experiences that I can share with you because I chose to stay in a beautiful riverside home of an elderly couple or in an apartment that is a reader's dream come true in Amsterdam simply beats any hotel stay I would have taken then. I got to meet some incredible people. Those people helped me find some remarkable places (and some awesome restaurants that I cannot compliment enough). You instantly feel like you are part of the locals (I got some useful tips on what not to do and how to find the best experiences).

Soon, I found myself making good friends, some of whom I have kept in touch with over the years. I would definitely go back to their homes the next time I am in town. Can't imagine a better way to explore the place.

Return of the Brand

Airbnb found themselves scaling fast.

They needed to change their identity to reflect the change that they have been experiencing.

In 2013, Brian Chesky sent a rather colorful letter to the entire staff at the firm. The main theme of the letter was an informal but straightforward message. It was about the advice that an investor once gave to the three founders. That advice was a cynical approach to doing business: from the perspective of the investor, every mom and pop startup eventually sells out for the big bucks. Chesky was not a sellout. And that was the message he wanted to express to his entire staff.

He wanted them to go the extra mile. Take responsibility for their actions and become embroiled in something big.

The letter even emphasized on the importance of organizational culture. It mentioned that the stronger the culture is at the company, the less mechanical corporate process is needed. That would imply that with a great culture, it is possible to give the staff a higher level of independence because they can be trusted to do the right thing.

He went on to commend employees that worked hard and put in the extra effort to make their service something truly different. He further explained that in the event that there is an unsatisfied customer, the staff member has autonomy to consider the best way to handle the client and his or her problems. He gave an example of an employee sending a package of a large teddy bear and a card as an opening to apologize to an aggrieved customer because of the negative experience he claimed to have had.

However, while showing the employees the type of culture that he would like them to uphold was a motivating gesture, he realized that he might need to make some big changes to the company itself. He wanted Airbnb to reflect the culture that he was talking about.

Hence, sometime later in 2013, the three founders began to consider their mission and vision. They wanted to send out a clear message and they knew that it was only through a rebrand that their company's image would appear "fresh" and "changed."

In order to get the right mission and align their objectives accordingly, they needed to discover the right elements that comprise the culture of the company.

The job of discovering the right elements was left to Douglas Atkin, who had joined the company as the Global Head of Community.

He was considering looking at the company's identity from a different perspective. He wanted Airbnb to communicate a message that would encompass the users as well. He wanted the hosts, the guests, the employees and the guests to become part of one cohesive identity. He wanted them to belong.

That was when the idea struck him.

He would reposition the company's identity around the concept of "belonging."

The founders warmed up to the idea.

It made perfect sense. After all, many things about Airbnb was about a sense of belonging. The host needs to feel comfortable with the application. They needed to belong to the world of Airbnb. Guests on the other hand always looked for a place where they belonged and were never made to feel unwelcome.

Employees should feel that they belong within the entire culture of Airbnb.

It fit the company's idea and the three founders decided to go ahead with the concept.

By mid-2014, the founders started making changes to its identity. It picked new colors for its brand, a combination of white and magenta. The logo itself was changed. It was given the name "The Bélo".

The log was a combination of four different symbols.

It features the symbol of a head, which is used to represent the people. These people that the logo highlights refer to the hosts, guests, employees, and anyone else who is part of the success of the company.

The second symbol in the logo is that of the location icon. This is an icon commonly used in almost every location or map application around the world. This symbol is used to reflect the many locations around the world that are part of Airbnb's service.

The third symbol used in the logo is that of a heart. That represents not just the love that is shared within the ever-growing community of Airbnb, but also the love the employees show for the company.

Finally, the last symbol used is the letter "A". This is, of course, a representative of the company name's first letter.

The company was definitely aiming to reach out to the emotional aspects of people. They wanted to make people feel that they are part of a bigger family.

Chesky then went on to introduce the rebrand in July 2014. He then wrote a blog entry on the company's website, talking about what the rebrand stood for.

He wanted Airbnb to stand for something much more than travel. He wanted it to represent the community and the relationships that formed between people.

He wanted the brand to be the one place where people went to feel a sense of "belonging", no matter what part of the world anyone lived in.

Of course, even their rebrand was met with a level of skepticism.

The people definitely loved the entire concept behind the rebrand. However, industry experts claimed whether it was really "belonging" that made people head over to Airbnb to find a place or the fact that Airbnb had some pretty cheap listings on their page.

There is a much deeper understanding to be gained by the term "belonging."

It was not about simply sitting with a person and enjoying a wonderful conversation over tea. It was much more than that. The idea that Chesky was trying to place in the minds of the people was the fact that they could belong in a particular neighborhood, city, a local hotspot of the country through the experiences that they would encounter by using Airbnb.

Nomads on the Run

Michael and Debbie Campbell are a retired couple from Seattle. In 2013, they decided to pack up their things and explore the world.

Now that does not sound like an original idea. In fact, it just sounds like what any retired couple would like to do.

But here is the twist to their story.

They decided to take out everything they could fit into suitcases and live only using Airbnb.

That's right.

By the year 2016, this couple had lived in nearly 125 listings on Airbnb. They had traveled to nearly 31 countries and they were planning on traveling to more.

What was their trick?

Frugality.

The couple were particular about what they spend on and kept a strict rule on how much they would spend every night, no matter what country they were planning to visit. Of course, some countries are expensive than others, but the overall idea is that if they were forced to spend more in one country, then they would lower their daily spending in another country.

They would usually book complete apartments for themselves. The apartment should come equipped with a few things that they are adamant about being included. They wanted their apartments to have a kitchen that had the necessary equipment and appliances for cooking and they required WiFi access to stay connected.

They usually stayed for a period of nine days in each apartment. However, they would extend their stay if the opportunity presented itself or if they really needed to manage their budget.

Their goal was not just to go on a vacation, but to actually live their daily lives. The only difference is that they would be doing it in other people's homes.

In 2015, the Campbell's sold their home in Seattle and used the money they received from the sale to continue on their journey. They are unsure of how long they would last, but they know one thing: they have no intention of stopping anytime soon.

The story of the Campbell's soon became a trending story. The New York Times picked up on the couple's travel tales and ran a piece on them. Pretty soon, they inspired other people to do the same, but not necessarily for the same length of time. Some would go on an exploratory tour around the world for a year; some would go for two years while still others would try out the idea for a few months.

Regardless of the duration one took in their travels, their main plan was to stay only in Airbnb listed rooms.

These people were termed "hipster nomads."

Another example is one of Kevin Lynch, a creative director who moved to Shanghai with his wife and two daughters.

Ever since he moved there, he had decided to avoid living in an apartment. He has chosen to use Airbnb to find places where he could stay. He has lived in more than 136 different rooms, stays, and other lodgings that he found only through Airbnb.

You might think that these nomads are just a small group of people. If you focus on those who live solely through Airbnb listings, then perhaps there are not many people who do that. However, there are many people who use Airbnb to live in multiple listings during a single trip or experience.

This shows the novelty that people are looking for. The chance to encounter unique things through a single platform.

Whatever can be said about the habits of the nomads, they are encouraging more and more people to try out their way of experiencing a country.

This has led to an increase in the nomad community, showing the faithful group of users on Airbnb.

These stories only serve to create a positive impression of the platform in the minds of the customers. This leads to more people joining the platform.

The Hosts

Airbnb does not have to focus on simply the nomad community. They need to pay attention to the hosts, which is something I had mentioned earlier.

However, there is a lot more to it than that.

You see, what makes the entire ecosystem of Airbnb work is the hosts that allow the usage of their rooms or space.

It is a tough challenge for Airbnb. After all, they not only have to ask more people to become part of their platform and rent out their rooms, but they have to also ask the people to make sure that the guests have a good experience.

All of this has to be done from the Airbnb headquarters in San Francisco, California.

This poses a problem for the company. They have to manage every aspect of their listings but they have no control over the hosts or the experience. In other words, Airbnb does not have any direct influence over their own inventory.

So how can they make sure that the hosts on their platform are giving a good enough experience?

This was something the company had to tackle and find a solution for.

During the initial period of the company's formation, the founders were aware of the problem of asking hosts to practically list their homes and ensure that the right service is provided.

It was not until millions of listings were made on the platform and many more were constantly added that the founders realized that they needed to do something to educate the hosts. Most importantly, whatever they were planning got do had to happen quickly.

And so, they hired Chip Conley.

Conley was the founder of Joie de Vivre, a hotel chain that was known for providing exemplary service to its guests.

His task was simple; he had to find a way to improve the experience that hosts provided to their guests. Okay, maybe his task was not that simple. Because he to make sure that he could communicate to as many hosts as possible.

That would definitely be a challenge as he had to find a way to reach out to millions of people.

However, Conley had a better idea. He traveled to nearly 25 countries where Airbnb was located and started giving presentations to the hosts. He invited them for conferences and spread marketing materials that they could use as guidelines.

Eventually, all the techniques that he communicated to the hosts were then included in Airbnb's guidelines to the hosts.

They encouraged the hosts to respond to the bookings as soon as possible, preferably within a 24-hour period

Before confirming a guest's booking, the hosts were encouraged to try and make sure that their services and hosting capabilities matched the expectations of the guest. Let me explain this with an example. If a guest is looking for the host to be present within the premises and if that would not be possible with the host, then it should be communicated to the guest before any booking has been made.

Hosts should also establish any house rules before confirming bookings. For example, if the host preferred the guest to not smoke within the room or pace premises, then this should be mentioned early and not after the guest completes the booking.

Rooms should be kept clean, especially the kitchen and the bathroom. Ensure that the beds and towels are maintained.

Conley also recommended trying to go the extra mile for the guest. Picking up the guest from the hotel is one way of showing a better experience. The host could also leave a welcome package for the guest.

These are just some of the ways that hosts can make sure that the guests are felt welcomed in their homes.

However, even after Conley's presentations and Airbnb's guidelines, they could not personally ensure if every host would follow the instructions.

That was where the rating and review system came in. Airbnb wanted the community to be the spokesperson for each and every listing on its platform.

What they wanted was not for the hosts to adhere to the guidelines presented by them as strictly as possible, but to make sure that they manage expectations and deliver a superb experience for the guests.

The rating system gave a chance for Airbnb to encourage better service from the hosts.

The founders also realized that they could also allow hosts' listings to be revealed on search rankings. This became a powerful tool to motivate the hosts. After all, who wouldn't want some extra promotion?

Hosts who were reviewed positively would find their listings appearing on the top of search results. This, in turn, gave their property better exposure and that attracted more guests to their listings.

But what if the hosts did not provide a good service? What if they were reviewed poorly? What happened when the guests declined too many bookings or even canceled numerous bookings made by guests?

Airbnb had a solution for that. If hosts were underperforming constantly, they would find their listings lowered considerably in the search rankings and could get their account banned.

For those hosts who continue to perform incredibly well; if they have provided at least 90% response rate, received a five-star review most of the time (according to Airbnb, there should be at least 80% five star reviews), ensured that cancellations occurred rarely and managed the guests' expectations, they would be rewarded by Airbnb.

These high-performing hosts would immediately receive the title of "Superhost."

Of course, this came with many benefits. For example, they would find their listings rising high in the search rankings. They would receive easy access to the customer service center, and could even attend any special events hosted by Airbnb in their country.

All of these benefits definitely worked their magic. Hosts began to compete for the Superhost status, ensuring that they not only provide an excellent service but also go out of their way to include something extra in the guest experience.

The Business of the Host

An average host earns more than $5,000 every year. However, there are many who have turned Airbnb's services into a full-fledged business. Many of these hosts have acquired multiple properties, apartments, and rooms around the city. Using Airbnb as a platform, some are earning as much as $10,000 per month.

Many people see Airbnb as a potential to start a business. They find out the best way to attract guests to a particular spot. This means that they look at what guests commonly book when they visit the city. They then look for similar places. Up on finding the apartment or space, they will completely renovate it for the guests.

That's when the booking starts coming through.

Eventually, after saving from the first property they had rented out, they would invest in another place to host. They would work on the second place, leading to the purchase of a third. This went on until they would have around four or five properties under them.

The number of places that each host owned depended on the place itself. If it is a small apartment and easy to maintain, then they might easily acquire at least four places.

However, if the space for rent was big - like a condo or a house - then the host would consider maintaining just two or three properties at most. With such big spaces, the price for staying in those places would also rise, netting the hosts a good side income.

Eventually, the hosts would bring in more people to manage the spaces while they looked for even more spaces to bring under their management. Some hosts even go to the extent of hiring assistants to do the cleaning at their spaces.

This was an effective idea for those who intended to make money through Airbnb. Of course, creating such an idea also meant maintaining the business. But for many people, the extra work was not a problem, especially considering the fact that they are practically earning a lot of money while doing it.

No matter how you want to look at it, Airbnb certainly gives more freedom to its hosts and allow them to explore multiple ways to make money off the platform.

The Horror!

But despite all the benefits they provide to the hosts and all the effort they go through to ensure that they create an incredible platform for everyone, there are always experiences that reveal the nasty side of the human race.

Mark and Star King, a Canadian couple had to return home from their holiday quickly. They were getting urgent notifications from their neighbors about a situation in their home. Up on their return, they found a scene straight out of their worst nightmares. The furniture and glass were all smashed. The couple discovered used condoms and fluids scattered all over their home. They had to invite the police to check the damages caused by the renters. Fortunately, they receive compensation through Airbnb's insurance policy.

In another story, a house was rented out to guests in Australia. This led to the guests causing disturbances to the neighbors. Eventually, the police were called in but they too had to retreat when the guests started throwing rocks at the officials. Eventually, a critical response squad was disposed to the area to bring a semblance of order to the situation.

In yet another incident, two women in Stockholm had listed their apartment on Airbnb. They received a booking and immediately left for their holiday trip after the completion of the booking. After their return, they discovered that their entire apartment had been used as a brothel, with used condoms discovered and other detritus discovered within the apartment premises.

With such stories, public opinion often wavers. People begin to believe the worst in a particular service by merely reading about certain incidents.

When the aforementioned situations were picked up by the media, they did nothing but tarnish the good reputation that Airbnb had built.

Most people had one question on their minds. Why had the company not already placed safety checks from the beginning? After all, they should have known that such incidents would be common on the platform.

Let us look at another incident that caught media attention for the wrong reasons.

In 2015, nineteen-year-old Jacob Lopez booked an apartment in Madrid using Airbnb. Shortly later, his mother began receiving texts that would probably be one of the worst situations that any parent could find himself or herself in.

Apparently, Jacob's host had locked him inside the apartment. The host, a transgender woman, began to request sexual favors from Lopez in return for his freedom.

Jacob immediately placed a call to his mother, who then decided to contact Airbnb for support. From her account, she claimed that the Airbnb employee she got in touch with would not provide her the address of the apartment or details of the host. Instead, she was given the number of local police. However, when she tried the number, she could not get through and when she contacted Airbnb, she was taken straight to voicemail.

Jacob Lopez then convinced his host to set him free, but not before the host assaulted him sexually.

The host claimed the entire incident was consensual. However, that did not matter for anyone who wanted to run an article on the story.

Regardless of what transpired that night, a bigger question came into play; how can Airbnb guarantee the safety of the guests?

After the Lope incident, Airbnb updated its policy and features to provide the ability for guests to contact the police in case of an emergency.

However, that did not sit well with the community. After all, why could they not provide the service before? Wasn't safety their primary concern? Didn't the company speak about a sense of belonging? What was the purpose of that if they could not keep the customers who use their service safe?

Airbnb responded back, showing the fact that such incidences were rare. They understood that sexual assault is a serious problem around the globe. But they pointed out the fact that there were many bookings in Madrid on that day; none of those bookings had led to any serious problems.

Safety was a vital concern for Airbnb. Chesky himself noted that if he so wished, he would like the percentage of horrific incidents on Airbnb to remain at 0%. However, that was not a guarantee he could provide and not a situation that is possible. With every product and service, there would always be the disasters that occur.

The one thing that Chesky aims to do is go the extra mile to ensure that such situations are handled well. He wants the customers to have compensation and their situations resolved. He believes in the idea that Airbnb is a high-trust community and he wants to maintain it that way.

However, here is a point to remember. There are disastrous situations that occur even in hotels. The only reason you do not hear of them is that the hotel industry is a large and long-living industry. When certain disastrous incidents happen in the hotel industry, there is usually a chance that it was not the first time that the incident took place. But due to the repetition of such incidences, people become immune to them. Unless the crisis is extreme (for example, a mass shooting), they usually do not get reported in the media.

Airbnb, on the other hand, is a young company. Sure, it has been in existence for several years. But the industry that it is part of is relatively new. This is why any incident on the platform feels fresh. Every time something happens, the chances of it escalating is high.

Keeping Things Safe

Such negative incidences were also why numerous investors had refused to invest in the company in its earlier stages. They felt that there were chances that someone could commit a serious crime within the premises of one of the listings on Airbnb. That could only spell catastrophe for the company and would harm the reputation immensely.

During the crisis management days of the company, the employees would find themselves living in the office for many days. They had to come up with solutions to fix the issues that plagued the system. They had to deal with angry customers and situations that seemed to spiral out of control.

These were the times that would prove to be crucial for the company. The efforts put in by the employees would eventually lead to the formation of the 24/7 call service center, the Host Guarantee (where a host was provided with an insurance policy of up to $1 million for compensation) and the presence of the special Trust and Safety Division within the company.

These actions would prove vital in establishing the company's good reputation and showing the public that Airbnb does indeed care about its users. Most importantly, the company wanted to project the idea that they were concerned about the safety of its guests and hosts, most particularly its hosts.

The Trust and Safety section would find itself growing. Over the years, it would go on to increase its team quickly. Currently, it includes a team of 250 people located in three countries; Dublin, Singapore, and the United States.

The Trust and Safety centers included numerous departments, each responsible for taking care of certain aspects of the Airbnb transaction process and the eventual experience of the guests and the hosts.

The center has a community-defense team. Their main role is to check if there have been cases of fraudulent activities on the platform if anyone is using false advertisements or listings if there have been cases of duplicate listings or any other form of suspicious activity on the platform. If any such situations are detected, then the community-response team takes over.

Their main role is to make certain that the crisis they are about to deal with is genuinely concerning or simply a minor error caused by the host or the guest. These minor errors could happen to first time hosts who are not fully aware of the system or how to work with the Airbnb mechanics.

Airbnb also includes a product team. This team uses data to discover if a particular listing has the potential to create a criminal situation or cause harm to either the guests or the hosts. The way the team does this is by looking at historical data and making comparisons with certain points. The tools developed by the engineers of the product team enables the team to take preventive measures if they are certain that a specific booking could cause problems to either or both parties involved in the transaction.

Apart from the above measures, the team has built in numerous features for the users themselves.

The company offers the feature of "Verified ID". This allows users to link their Airbnb profile to other sources of personal information. These sources of information may entail uploading an official government-provided ID; providing an email address or phone number; or linking their online profiles (like Google, LinkedIn, or Facebook account) with their respective Airbnb accounts. Visitors with different kinds of IDs can use all of those IDs to provide their account with an enhanced threshold of security. This security makes it easier to authenticate their real beings to hosts. Presenting an Identity Card, Driver's License, or a Passport; connecting social media accounts, and verifying a real phone number or email address all help to facilitate the development of a verified ID for any user of the platform.

The company has also come up with a private messaging

system between guests and hosts. If there is any kind of communication before bookings, the hosts and guests have to make them via this dedicated system. In this case, hosts can be relieved in realizing that every communication they engage in is secure and safe since it is happening on a protected platform. Only registered members of Airbnb can use this messaging system and all potential clients need to present their official credit cards as well as upload their profile photos as a bare minimum before getting access to the system. Via this system, the company can trace any communication and they proactively take efforts to identify fraudulent or suspicious actions. This communication system is used to make sure that both parties - guests and hosts - attempt to confirm the conditions, and any other pertinent information, about the listing before approving any booking. However, while this communication system provides better access for the users, the company discourages the sharing of personal information related to bank account details, credit card information, and other financial data.

Airbnb also allows hosts to develop their property rules. These rules set the expectations for the visitors. Hosts can display these rules on the company listing pages where potential visitors can check them prior to booking a reservation. The rules could any form of rules, including notifying the guests about the areas where they can smoke, whether drinking is allowed within property premises, whether the hosts accept pets or even the maximum number of people allowed within a property. While setting rules do not exactly guarantee the safety of the hosts, it does give the hosts a degree of freedom when creating their listings. This allows them to reduce the potential of attracting guests whom they might find unwelcome within their premises.

The company presently requires further verification when its clients log in using new devices like phones, tablets, or computers – as it always happens with other online services like banking. When users sign up for the first time, the Airbnb system remembers the device a customer has used and it enables him/her to log in next time from the same device. Such features are known as "multi-factor authentications". The aim of this form of security is to ensure that the right person has access to a specific account. Airbnb forwards a one-time distinct verification code to the user's email account or phone number. After entering the code through the new device, the users can access their device. If they make use of another device, they have to follow the same verification steps again.

When Things Are beyond Control

Despite the many regulations that Airbnb sets up to protect its hosts and guests, there are incidents that occur that may be beyond anyone's control. Airbnb might be able to provide the right kind of assistance to most scenarios. But what happens when a situation occurs where an accident leads to mortal injury or even death.

Imagine this.

Someone books a room through Airbnb. They find out that the space has a rope swing in the backyard and are excited by the feature. Once they reach the place, they are eager to try out the swing

When they climb up on the swing, it seems sturdy enough. They begin using the swing but a while later, the tree limb that holds the swing break and falls down, hitting the person on the head. This causes a brain injury, leading to a person's death.

That is what exactly happened to Zak Stone's father.

And that did not sit well with Stone. In a blog entry, he described in detail the event that led to his father's death.

Incidences like that are beyond Airbnb's control, at least according to the company. It feels that it cannot be held liable for the damages caused by such incidences. Despite its many safeguards, there are bound to be situations where the host may not follow the strict regulations they like to impose.

You can a disclaimer on its website as well that notifies the users that Airbnb has no control over the actions of the users. If there is a violation of its policies, then it might lead to a permanent cancellation of the account.

The founders are aware of these situations and do their best to monitor listings where certain aspects or features of the home may not be how it was pictured in the listing.

However, they can only do so much. Chesky might seem idealistic. His vision for a sense of belonging that the company advertises includes bringing together people across the world. He does believe that every incident that leads to personal harm (or death in a couple of cases) for the guests saddens him immensely.

However you want to look at the scenario, these incidence gave ammunition to the hotel industry and other opposition of Airbnb. You see, hotels have to follow a strict code of conduct and safety regulations. Every country has its own rules for the hotels, but it more or less involves the safety of the guests under the hotel's care.

There are safety standards that are related to fire prevention, where the hotel has to have fire extinguishers placed in a certain manner and in certain numbers. Fire extinguishers should also be placed within a certain distance of each other, allowing anyone to reach them if easily if necessary.

Other forms of health and safety standards could come in the form of hygiene.

One of the key requirements when opening hotels in any country are to show the governments of that country that the hotels can show that food handling and preparation are done with a certain set standard.

In fact, such standards ensure that the food is safe to eat.

In similar ways, there are standards for many aspects of a hotel's services.

With Airbnb and other related services do not go through the same standards that are placed on the hotel.

If you go through the company's requirements for the hosts, then you will notice that the hosts have to make sure that there is a fire alarm system, smoke detector and all of the exposed wirings must be fixed.

While that sounds good on paper, it does not exactly guarantee the fact that anyone would actually follow the rules. It only lays down the criteria, but it cannot guarantee actions taken by the hosts themselves.

Now example, let us take the case of Cecil Hotel located in Los Angeles. In 2013, the police discovered the body of 21-year old student Elisa Lam, who had apparently been murdered at the hotel.

In similar ways, you simply have to perform a quick Google search and you will discover cases involving bodily harm and deaths in hotels, from suicides to accidents to murders.

All of these deaths talk about how – no matter the safety precautions that are taken in any place – catastrophes can happen anywhere.

It is for this reason that the hotel industry is not opposing so openly to Airbnb. They understand that within their premises, accidents can occur. They are only one major and terrible incident away from appearing in the newspapers.

It is true that no matter whose house we enter using Airbnb, we are placing ourselves to a degree of harm. This is because we are not sure who the hosts are; they are strangers after all. Most importantly, because of the fact that the hosts are unknown, we are not certain of their motives as well.

This the same in hotels as well. No matter how safe we think hotels are, there are always chances of encountering a harmful incident.

The only difference between a hotel and Airbnb is that we know that when we are in a hotel, we can head over to the front desk or perhaps even security – if they are available – and seek assistance regarding a problem. In the case of Airbnb, this may not be the case because the role of security and the front desk or even the staff is taken up by the host of the place you are living in. This makes the entire situation fairly complicated.

In such situations, we rely on the service provider to provide us with the assistance that we require.

With Airbnb, the company has a history of responding poorly to certain situations. This can be attributed to the fact that the company has never dealt with situations like that before. Because every new incident is relatively fresh (and occurring during the growth phase of the company), it settles in the minds of the customers far longer. When situations happen in hotels, one often thinks of the individuals behind the incident. For example, if an incident led to the death of a guest in a hotel, then one would focus on the people who caused the death. How did it happen? Who was responsible for it?

People do not tend to blame the hotel because it incorporates rules and regulations and in the case of the aforementioned incident, those rules and regulations were compromised.

When the same situation occurs in an Airbnb listing and when the community asks the same questions, they often blame Airbnb because the company does not have a physical presence like hotels to represent their rules and regulations. It seems like they are handing over the responsibility over to the individuals who host the people within their property premises.

This is one of the reasons why many people often feel that Airbnb is directly responsible for any incident that occurs in a host's property.

The Law of the Land

We looked briefly at how laws can affect a company such as Airbnb, especially when it concerns rental conditions within the country that the company is operating in. In 2010, Chesky received a call from a particular host. The host mentioned to Chesky that there was going to be a new law enacted within the city of New York.

This immediately grabbed the attention of Chesky. However, he had no idea about the law and how he was going to deal with it. It definitely seemed like an alien concept to him.

After hearing about the new law from the host, Chesky

considered numerous options. He thought of dealing with the new situation himself.

Before that, he decided to get in touch with numerous people and get their advice on the matter. One of the advisors recommended that he hire a lobbyist to represent the company and then face the various lawmakers. Chesky could not understand why the company would need a lobbyist.

In his mind, he was hiring someone to speak to the lawmakers because the lawmakers would not talk to Chesky directly. It was not a matter he was used to.

After much searching, he narrowed down his focus to a firm called Bolton-St. Johns. While working with the company Chesky realized that the laws enacted were about the rental conditions in New York. These laws would be set up within the month and Chesky had only that much time to prepare for them. He had to go through a crash course to deal with everything that might be thrown against the company.

What Chesky and the rest of the founders were about to discover was that their idea of allowing people to rent out their homes to others would be in violation of the laws and rules in many cities, countries, and even regions around the world.

That was a hard blow for the team. It was not as if they did not expect it, but it still was something they were hoping not to face.

Imagine if the very idea that your company works on finds itself under attack.

Things were looking grim for the team.

Even the laws themselves were not set for the entire region.

Sometimes, they would differ between two towns and even two areas. This gave the team a whole new level of complexity to deal with. They had to hire teams in different countries to deal with different situations.

What made matters worse was the fact that even hosts were somehow trying to break the rules as well. They would avoid local taxation by not informing local authorities, they would completely ignore zone regulations and building maintenance requirements, and in some cases, create disturbances in the local community.

Airbnb set itself to the task.

It would not back down from the challenges, but it would definitely require assistance.

The founders would then work with local regulators, who would assist the team in amending rules of the region. They would then set about to make the service legal in those cities and regions, provided that certain laws were obeyed. Of course, that is a guarantee that Airbnb cannot provide to the government, as controlling each and every activity of the various hosts on its platform is next to impossible. Nevertheless, they created unique regulations for each region they operated in, ensuring that the hosts were aware of these regulations.

While this was not exactly the response that local law authorities were looking for, they soon realized that this is the best that the company can do; they cannot directly influence every person's actions.

Over the years, the company would itself creating vital agreements and policies regarding its operations in numerous locations around the world. Some of these locations include

Paris, London, Shanghai, and Chicago. The company would then find itself approaching many other countries, trying to replicate the successes.

But not all regions or cities are as open to changes. Places such as Barcelona and New York involve lawmakers who are refusing to budge, despite every reason and assurances provided to them. They do not intend to change the laws for any entity, regardless of how well they can work together.

Of course, the same laws apply to other short-term rental companies in the world. The difference lies in the severity of the laws faced by these companies.

You see, Airbnb is massive. It is only growing each day and this growth brings it under the scrutiny of numerous entities. While other companies have fewer options on their platform and do not necessarily provide all the options as Airbnb does (for example, many of the platforms simply provide alternatives to hotels, and not necessarily compete with them, even when regards to the prices of the rentals), Airbnb has positioned itself to be easily targeted by lawmakers and governments.

One of the major battles that Airbnb faced was in the city of New York. According to the company itself, most of its market share comes from New York. Not surprisingly, hotels also have an incredibly high market share in the same city. After all, it has been recorded that the city with the highest number of visitors in New York, with over an estimated number of more than 56.7 million visitors in the year 2016 alone. When lawmakers became aware of this, they created a new law. According to this law, individuals in New York could not advertise their property on any platform, whether online or offline, if it met the following conditions:

- They were renting out the place for less than thirty days

- They were not physically present when the guest was inside property premises

This was practically the entire purpose of Airbnb. They could allow hosts to rent out their spaces and apartments for a short duration and they did not necessarily have to be inside their property at all times. When Airbnb heard about the new law, they knew that they had to take decisive action against it. It was not an easy feat, after all, the majority of the lawmakers were in support of the new law.

Airbnb decided to file a lawsuit against the city, through which they got the city to settle. However, the entire matter caused a great deal of concern for the company and even revealed how much of an impact one single law can make to the entire process of Airbnb.

Let us look back a couple of years earlier as well and examine another situation. It was the year 2014 and Airbnb was aware of another threat to its company from the enactment of laws.

This time, the company had a different approach to things. Instead of hiring people to change the laws, they hired people to change the perception of their company. Signs and messages were spread all across New York City. You could spot them in subways, catch them being promoted online on various social platforms, and even see ads about them in televisions. All of these messages had one common denominator; "NYC Supports Airbnb."

The company realized that sometimes, in order to show public officials the impact they have on the community and city at large, they needed to take the support of the people themselves to create any form of impact.

They sent out people to seek support from the public, often approaching them in person and seeing if they would like to pledge their support for the company.

By June of 2014, the company's goal was to collect at least 10,000 votes, or pledges, from the public. This was its aim to show the city that its residents were in full support of the company and its values. This was a way to show everyone that despite the controversies that the company faces, it has created a strong following of people who, at their core, understand what the company stands for.

It seemed like a daunting task. How are they going to find 10,000 people who can provide their support to the company? Where are they going to target? Whom are they going to target?

Of course, they could always ask the users on their platform for support, but the whole point was to show that apart from those already using their platform, people were accepting the entire idea of having Airbnb in their city.

When they first stepped out to meet the residents of New York, they would walk over to people and ask them if they were open to the idea of Airbnb.

After the campaign took headway, they managed to raise 2,000 pledges to support the campaign. Eventually, that 2,000 turned to 5,000.

As their campaign continued, they noticed that more and more people were part of the program, giving their vocal support and sometimes adding their voices on social platforms.

The petition to gain support from the masses acquired its 10,000 pledges. However, what happened next was something that even the founders could not have predicted.

By the end of the campaign, they had received more than 20,000 pledges and support from the residents of New York.

This was better than the target that they had set for themselves.

AirbnbNYC became a popular group and messages of "NYC supports Airbnb" were cropping up everywhere in the city.

While this was not enough to turn the attention of the lawmakers toward their opinions, it was enough to gain traction in their campaign to allow laws that provide the required freedom to Airbnb hosts.

Nick Pappas, spokesperson for Airbnb talked about how a lot of the people in the city were not aware of the benefits that Airbnb provides them and the measures that the company takes to ensure the safety of its users. He wanted the community to be more aware of Airbnb can provide not just for individuals, but also for the visitors of the city.

It was true that people were often subjected to the news that they viewed, often showing one side of the story. Airbnb aimed to change that and provide information that could help its reputation.

Some people were of the opinion that the entire campaign was a mere PR stunt to gain credibility and acquire support for Airbnb. This support would go a long way when Airbnb needed it, especially in their attempts to change the law to provide more leeway for their activities. Others thought that the move was important for more people to be aware of Airbnb's side of the story.

The company had a voice and they deserve to reach out to people to hear them.

Whatever side you take, the tactic worked for the company. As more and more people began to be aware of the situation and of Airbnb's part in the recent circumstances that affected the company, public officials were forced to acknowledge that they had to change the laws.

However, this need to lobby for getting laws changed would not just be a matter that would end in a year.

Over the years, Airbnb would find itself in the middle of similar situations numerous times.

In 2017, the company had to spend more than $400,000 on lobbying in the just the first six months alone. This expense shows the degree to which it has to go to ensure that the laws do not abruptly change. They want to make sure that the capacity to host exists in all the cities that it operates in, especially in those places where it has a strong influence.

We just talked about lobbying but haven't even mentioned what it means. So let's get down to it.

You see, lobbying is the act of trying to influence the government or members of the government to change a regulation, take part in an activity, or influencer others for the benefit of a particular organization or individual.

After reading that, you might automatically assume that it definitely sounds like something nefarious.

After all, influencing people? That sounds like corruption.

Does that mean that Airbnb is involved in some pretty nefarious deeds?

Not so fast.

Here is the thing that most people do not know about lobbying. There are a lot of organizations, including non-profit and humanitarian entities, which engage in lobbying. That does not make them inherently "bad", for lack of a better term. It just means that they want to make certain that their actions do not face too much opposition.

Which is, why, lobbying does not represent an act that constitutes a crime. In fact, it is an act protected by the First Amendment. It is the right of the citizen to petition the government.

By taking that into context, we can get a clear picture of the actions taken by Airbnb. We understand that their business model is not illegal, yet certain laws prevented them from conducting their services freely. Which is why it was up to them to convince lawmakers of their services and find out ways to allow the law to give their hosts the freedom to rent out their spaces.

Airbnb's experience in New York clearly highlights the importance of being prepared. The company was not aware of how many challenge it could face and from what angles. It underestimated the effect that the law and governments can have on its business.

It definitely was an eye-opener for the company. Having realized that if they threatened the existing nature of industries and companies, they might face serious backlash, they proceeded with their business much more carefully. More importantly, the company understood the lives that it was capable of affecting with its services. A sense of belonging sounds like a nice motto to have and an incredible goal to follow, but it does come with a set of responsibilities.

Here is something that you should be aware of; the practice of short-term rentals was nothing new. It had existed for a long time and was even popular on sites like Craigslist (even newspapers used to run ads for rentals). So what exactly changed with Airbnb?

When you look at a company like Airbnb, you have to realize that they survive on having more hosts on their platform. That means increasing the number of short-term rentals in a particular city. Previously, people had to navigate to a particular section of the local or online classifieds and then check out the properties listed there. They then had to look through the already limited number of spaces available and choose the one that fit their needs (more often than not, it never did fit their needs). With such a limited number of rental spaces strewn across the city, most hotels and governmental institutions did not pay attention. It was hardly worth noticing after all.

With Airbnb (and the ease it provides for numerous individuals to create rental spaces), the number of short-term rentals was not in the negligible number. The rentals had grown tremendously.

This obviously caught the attention of city officials, governmental and municipal bodies, and other public officials. And every time Airbnb had a victory, they would only serve to heighten the intensity at which these officials would target the company.

Take, for example, the case in the year 2012 in New York.

Now, before we dive right into the specifics of the case, here is something else you should be aware of that year. It had come to Airbnb's attention that there was a crackdown on a number of the rental spaces listed on its website.

It so happened that one of the victims of this crackdown was a web designer who had rented out his apartment to a woman from Russia while he had left the city on a holiday. He was out of the city for just a few days, but when he returned, he realized that officials had slapped a shocking $40,000 fine on his landlord.

Of course, he took the case to the court and eventually, Airbnb had to step in to explain things further. They mentioned the fact that the web designer had only rented out just one room in his apartment and not the entire apartment, so the fine of $40,000 was not exactly justified.

The court ruled in favor of the Airbnb host and to the company, it was a victory. However, this only led to an increase in the commitment of the Airbnb opposition. To them, this was hardly a fair result.

This led to a sort of anti-Airbnb movement that gained strength as time passed. It consisted of numerous city officials, representatives of the hotel industries, activists, and numerous other members of the governmental and municipal bodies. These officials began to take the help of people who found that Airbnb hosts interrupted their daily routine. Every time a host would create a disturbance in their vicinity, the officials would get them to sign a petition or raise a complaint against the company. It was as though both sides were trying to dismantle the efforts of the other through support, lobbying and various form of marketing.

People were made aware of the problems that the company can cause to residents. One of these problems could be the presence of safety issues that could affect the normality of the residents of a building. Airbnb listings were also often named as the "illegal hotels", creating the idea that they were not allowed to function in the city. Unlike other organizations who had the approval of the city and the government, Airbnb was not under any such regulations.

The Copycats

One of the problems with a business like Airbnb is that it often leads to many more short-term rental businesses opening up. While this may not sound like a bad idea, it does encourage everyone else to jump in on the concept of renting out their homes as well.

Housing units, homeowners, landlords, real estate companies, and anyone else who would like to take the opportunity to make some money through the process of renting out their homes for a short duration. This creates a problem. When such actions start increasing, the government officials interfere to put an end to it. Which is why, for all the problems that these situations create, someone has to be held accountable. In this case, the fault falls entirely on Airbnb.

While it is true that the company has repeatedly mentioned that they do not encourage such behavior from the public or any other institution, they cannot help prevent them from happening. Airbnb has managed to assist local authorities in finding people or businesses engaged in short-term rentals as a sign of good faith. But that does not help the fact that they were eventually responsible for popularizing the idea.

In the early days of Airbnb's operations in New York, it drew a lot of people imitating its services in the city.

You only have to perform a quick Google search for the name Robert "Toshi" Chan and you will probably find a few articles about a man that managed hundreds of short-term rental apartments all over the city. Chan was managing these apartments illegally and promoting them on Airbnb and other websites. He would often provide multiple apartments for short-term stays but would only provide a rent to his landlord that is only a small portion of the money he makes off of renting the apartments.

Eventually, Chan was sued and he lost the settlement, shelling out $1 million as payment for his actions.

You might think that such an action might have put an end to the acts. However, that was not the case.

Chan's situation was but one of many others who operated in a similar manner.

Soon, there would be a trend of people who would go on to start creating listings on Airbnb and multiple sites. Some listings saw people divide their apartment into different sections and rent out each section separately. With that, they began earning more money than the rent they were paying to their landlords. Eventually, these tenants were evicted from their apartments, but not before the situation was noted down by local officials who needed the ammunition to oppose Airbnb in any way that they can.

The incidents involving landlords evicting their tenants from the houses became a common occurrence not just in New York, but in other parts of the country.

Airbnb realized that the problem had escalated. Their usual tactics to gain support would not work this time.

Instead, they resorted to a much more bold approach to getting their message across to the people. They created a TV spot.

In the TV spot, named "Meet Carol", an African American single mother started using her apartment for guests after she had lost her job. She can be seen making the space livable for the guests by cleaning out the sheets and preparing breakfast.

If you do get a chance, simply search "Meet Carol" in your search bar and check out the ad. It might give you an impression of the direction Airbnb was taking in their marketing campaigns.

The idea behind the campaign was to show that despite everything, Airbnb truly helps people. It gives people a chance to make a small business out of their homes, especially when they do not have a job or are in need of finances.

The company agrees that many of the hosts on its platform use Airbnb to make the most of their listing and earn a living through them. They claim that these listings help families pay bills and keep a steady flow of income into their homes.

Using this strategy, it moved on to other countries. It talked about how its listings bring awareness about many areas of the world to tourists. This brings in more businesses to these areas and that only allows the people living in those areas to earn a better income.

You only have to head over to their website and you will find many reports that claim the company "promotes sustainable tourism."

In fact, in one such report published on May 29, 2018, you will see that they expound on the fact that their community helps in creating sustainable growth for everyone, from the community itself to other local businesses.

Airbnb believes in the idea that it is benefiting a lot of people through its services, especially in countries where tourism contributes to a big portion of its national income.

This tactic seemed to resonate with the audiences. They understood the value of allowing a community to thrive. They saw that Airbnb were promoting good values and good business practices around the world. It definitely got the people's attention focused on the company and their support for the company's goals.

However, what it set out to do, it could not achieve. The main purpose of the entire campaign was to get the attention of the opponents of Airbnb. The company wanted to show them that what it was doing benefited a lot of people, despite every terrible incident that occurred in the past.

It was a way for the company to place itself in the good graces of the opponents. Sadly, they did not get to succeed in their endeavor.

Their opponents' stance against the company intensified. They began to blame the company for using sentimental and emotional campaigns to manipulate the minds of the masses. They claimed the company was trying to divert the attention from the areas where it had to focus its attention to other areas. According to the opponents, the company was doing this in order to dilute the intensity of the mistakes committed by it.

New York, New York

I know. We are focusing on New York quite a lot. But to understand the nature of the problem, it is best to examine the city in which they not only have a large share, but also some of the largest problems.

We can analyze the problem from both ends and realize that

whatever stance you take on the matter, both sides of the argument have valid points.

Let us examine the opposition and see what they think of the entire problem and also see if we can agree to some of the points that they highlight.

The first thing that they mention is the fact that when you provide guests who visit the city keys to a house, then you are leaving the responsibility of the apartment or home with the guest. This could lead to much bigger problems later on. Let us assume that the guests do not lock their doors properly. This might lead to theft within the homes or worse, someone using it for nefarious purposes. Furthermore, many apartments do not provide the safety measures that you find in hotels and other governmentally and city approved lodgings. These apartments do not have sprinkler systems or security devices such as cameras to monitor the activity that takes place within its premises.

Let us assume that one of the guests did not stub out the cigarette inside the room. This leads to a fire within the apartment premises. Because there are no safety features installed in the building, the fire could soon spread to other apartments as well, putting the lives of other tenants and residents at risk.

It is, of course, easy to blame the guest for this. However, on a typical day, the apartment would not have been given out to strangers. It was only the option of making it a rental space that gave the owner the opportunity to give it to someone for a temporary stay.

In New York (and in probably many parts of the world), people protect their personal space. When tourists tend to place their luggage where they should not, dispose of plastic or other items on roofs or even create noise in the middle of the night, it tends to create havoc into the lives of the residents.

It just shows how these tourists do not respect the presence of the residents and the community that they have maintained for so long.

However, the opposing sides of the argument are less interested in these disturbances than other reasons that affect the bottom line on their profit margins.

One of the arguments lies in the fact that when more and more units become part of Airbnb, the remaining units have to cope with rental increases.

This is how it works. Let us assume that an apartment has been given away for rent. Remember how I mentioned that in some cases, Airbnb hosts end up earning more than what they pay for the rent? Let us apply the same logic for this example. When the landlord discovers, he or she is forced to adopt one of two measures:

- The landlord evicts the tenant permanently from the premises
- The rent of the apartment is increased to match the earnings of the tenant.

However, the landlord cannot increase the rent of one person without increasing the rent of the other apartments.

Another reason is the fact that having numerous apartments listed on Airbnb creates a shortage of available units. This means that there is not enough supply to match the demand. When that happens, city officials are forced to increase the rents of many units to keep up with the demand.

These are all sound arguments when you think about them. They definitely put the pressure on Airbnb to come up with a viable solution in order to satisfy not just its goals, but also calm the opposition. Definitely does not sound like an easy task considering the fact that the opposition is adamant about their stance and refuse to accept any reason to budge.

But Airbnb believes that the entire situation can be looked at in another manner.

They believe that even if they have removed certain units, which does not fully contribute to the increase in rents across the city.

When you look at apartments, you often think of one thing: construction. You see, when the city constructs more buildings, it helps in creating more spaces for people to live in. The number of different types of buildings that they have to create depends on the demand. However, in many cases, this is usually not how it happens.

Many people flock to the city in search of better jobs and opportunities. Colleges receive many students from across the country and you often find migrants arriving in the city to study at numerous universities. Because of the influx of such a large population, you obviously have an increase in the demand for more housing or even spaces to live.

To help with this problem, the city has to focus on creating more affordable housing projects. This is done so that it can help all the people who do not have a high source of income.

But what is happening is that cities focus on creating more upscale and high-end housing and apartment projects. This is because of the level of investments that these apartments attract. Meanwhile, those who really require affordable places to stay are not able to find enough places to move into. This creates an imbalance and a shift in the demand-supply curve.

There are more people who want to find inexpensive rental spaces and there are less affordable rental spaces for them.

This creates a tough competition among the various projects that are already set in place. For this reason, many apartments find their rents being increased in order to find the right resident to move in.

As the demand is higher, the rents increase even more.

Airbnb is clearly aware of this and is using the facts to show the opposition that the fault cannot be placed solely on them. There are numerous other factors that come into play when considering the idea of an increase in rents.

The faster than Airbnb grew, the more opposition that it faced. In fact, it seemed like the tensions were escalating. The opposition was reluctant to shift their perspectives and consider any other alternatives to the beliefs that they had already set up. To Airbnb, that situation became frustrating that they had to resort to even more marketing stunts to show their good name. This, in turn, did not work in their favor.

In fact, they even got an actor and fellow investor in the company Ashton Kutcher to side with them. He did and even composed a lengthy letter to public officials, giving reasons to show how the company were not in the business of causing harm.

On the other hand, this did nothing to appease the law officials. They wanted to make sure that Airbnb received every bit of penalty that is due to them. They feel that Airbnb cannot operate above the law and that the only way that they should be allowed to continue is if they can either follow the rules and regulations or stop their business entirely.

Do You Want To Be a Host?

The challenge that Airbnb had right now was to create hosts.

Actually, let us step back a little.

See, at this point, Airbnb was going through numerous battles against the city. Officials had enacted laws that would prevent one single apartment from being listed twice. This affected the business model of Airbnb and they had to find new ways to create hosts in the city. How can it accomplish this without catching the ire of lawmakers and other public officials in the city? Seemed like a difficult task indeed.

The company also aimed to create new hosts in a way that reflected the message that it was showing – a sense of belonging.

So there were two challenges that the company was facing:

How can they allow news hosts to come onto the platform and then represent the entire ideology of Airbnb?

What can they do to make sure that one host can only list one home and still be able to profit from it?

It was a situation that required the founders to come up with some intuitive plans.

They were used to facing challenges head and making sure that they come out with some incredible solutions. Will they be able to do the same here knowing that they could place themselves in jeopardy with the city again.

Eventually, the founders came up with an idea. Previously,

they used to let the hosts manage the properties on their own. They gave full permission for the hosts to promote their spaces to the guests and then make a profit out of it.

However, this time, they realized that perhaps they could work with the landlords to make sure that their ideas come to fruition.

In many places around the city, the problem lies with the fact that apartment landlords do not allow the tenants to list their apartments on Airbnb. This definitely seemed to be a problem with the landlords. Many of these landlords did not want to entertain the idea of short-term rentals in their properties because:

- It broke the rules and regulations they establish for the apartments.
- It also goes against local regulations and hence, it creates problems for the landlords
- The landlords are the once get receive a hefty fine and bear the full brunt of the law

Now there are two kinds of landlords; those that own a single building or a few buildings building in the city and those that own a list of buildings strewn across the city.

Those that control multiple buildings are usually companies that have properties all over the country. In fact, they probably own hundreds of thousands of properties in various states.

Therein lies the potential for Airbnb.

Their job was not to get in touch with these companies and change their minds about allowing Airbnb listings within their premises. Not an easy task with all the back-and-forth with the law and public officials that Airbnb had been engaged in for a few years.

However, if they manage to get the companies on their side, they not only can begin allowing hosts to list their homes and spaces but also get access to numerous other properties that they did not have access to before.

It seemed like a double win for them

Of course, the first part of the problem was to convince the companies.

Over the course of the next few years, Airbnb has been going to many of these companies and trying to make alliances with them.

In 2016, one of the companies created what they called a special agreement with Airbnb that was named as "Airbnb Friendly Building Program."

According to this program, owners of property can definitely sign up for an agreement with Airbnb. This will allow these owners to create listings on the site to promote its homes.

In return for the listings, the companies that manage these properties have the freedom to enact certain rules in regards to the property. For example, they can declare what areas of the property can be used for smoking and drinking. They can mention the hours during which there should be no noise outside the homes. Additionally, they also get a share of the revenue made by the owners.

Moreover, while the bookings are made through Airbnb, the company will share information about those bookings with the companies. This information does not entail providing details of the individuals who have made the bookings. Rather, the information provides details of which property is in higher demand and what has been charged for each booking.

This allows the company to make informed decisions about their properties. For example, they can find out which property to promote in the market and what properties need either an increase or reduction in the rent.

This helps the landlords and the companies both. The landlords are happy because their properties get filled up and companies are happy because not only are there rules placed on the properties, but they receive a small portion of the revenue.

It seemed that Airbnb had found a solution, for however long that may last.

As partnerships seem to be working for the company, they have decided to take this one step further. They plan to host numerous events to promote the idea of partnerships, allowing more companies to join them. These companies also include real estate companies, who develop new properties, which would benefit Airbnb even further.

However, these plans focus on places other than New York. After all, if the company were to try something like that in New York City, they would not only face serious backlash but also come to the attention of the city who would not mind taking the company through another court case.

The founders hope that by spreading the idea to various other locations around the country, they will be able to change the minds of the lawmakers in New York City. Lofty ambitions, but one has to start somewhere to get somewhere.

Mark Your Scars and Get Back In the Fight

Most experts believe that Airbnb will receive the freedom that it is seeking in many places around the world. Just a few years ago, in 2015, it was faced with one of the strictest restrictions on its listing. In the city of Santa Monica, city officials were in favor of a new law that outright banned the presence of any short-term rentals that allow guests to stay within apartments or other lodgings less than thirty days. This was a major blow to Airbnb. Most of their business comes from the fact that they can allows hosts to rent out their spaces for even a single day should they want to.

What many countries do not know is that the demand for Airbnb is high. Even if they pass bans today, the chances that they will free up regulations for Airbnb to continue is slightly high.

There might definitely be more restrictions placed on the company in order for it to continue. Regardless, consumer demand is high and city officials and governments might find a way to allow Airbnb to continue its presence within their country.

You can see the way consumer interest in the company has increased. There are more people that support the company than people who are against it.

It is obvious, it provides them with the opportunity to make use of their homes or properties when they are not using it.

What about the hotel industry. No matter how you look at it, they are being affected as well. Won't they step up and lead the fight against the company (or at least take part in it)?

Of course. There is no doubt about the fact that the hotel industry would like to place in their weight on the issue and try to influence the outcome. With millions of homes now under Airbnb, there is a large portion of the market that is affected.

With the fact that Airbnb is launching new features that allow people with more spending power to enjoy luxurious settings, it definitely seems like the company is engaging the hotel industry directly.

This might not sit well with the hotels. When they realize that part of the population they are targeting has switched sides to Airbnb, there might definitely be consequences to that.

If you are wondering why these new offerings would disrupt the hotel industry, then think of it this way.

You have a hotel that provides you some of the exquisite rooms. Of course, these rooms are expensive, but you feel that with all the features and facilities that the hotel is offering, spending a little extra is worth it.

But what happens when you can spend the same but get yourself an entire house? What if you could get yourself a beautiful two-bedroom apartment with incredible views of the city? What if it was a luxury condo?

These are some of the questions that the hotel industry might have to face in the future.

Of course, with Airbnb already established in the market, the idea of introducing luxury homes and condos might become a seamless process. This is because having more innovations on the platform might be readily welcome by the community. It is like Apple introducing the Pods, their wireless earpieces. Sure, it seemed different but it was a feature that was immediately accepted by the consumer base because the innovation related to what Apple has always been doing; creating cool tech.

In a similar manner, the idea of introducing new types of properties might be readily welcomed by the Airbnb community and by millions of hosts worldwide, much to the dismay of hotels.

Let's not forget the new programs that the company constantly launches.

Yeah, there are more that you should know about.

Apart from the ones mentioned above, the company is also in the process of launching "Business Travel Ready" program. You might have guessed it at this point that not everyone can become part of this program. This means that the eligibility goes to a select few who provide certain features to the guests.

For example, if a host provides WiFi connection, a clean environment to live in, iron for the clothes, shampoo and toiletries, they instantly become eligible for this program.

When the hosts join the program, they are given a logo. This logo allows them to differentiate themselves in the listings.

You might think that you have seen this feature somewhere else and you are right if you guessed the answer as websites that list properties.

This definitely is a way for Airbnb to provide the rental companies they are typing up with more incentives to partner with the company. By 2016, the company claimed that more than fifty thousand companies signed up for the program.

It was incredible.

By simply providing more features to the rental companies, they had given them reasons to become part of the platform. With this move, they can also gain the support of these rental companies. This might prove beneficial to the company in the future when they find opposition from city officials and other members of the government.

A Home Away From Home

When we look at Airbnb, we forget that it also has competition.

That is a subject that we had never broached upon, but it does not mean that there is limited competition for the company to face.

One of Airbnb's strongest competitors was HomeAway.

So why isn't HomeAway fighting against oppositions and legislation? Why aren't they more popular than Airbnb? After all, they have been in the market for far longer than Airbnb.

Both of these platforms used to boast a significant amount of users when it comes to the guests and the hosts. Both of these also give opportunities for the guest to find a listing and then book their rental depending on the location in the world. Hosts are welcomed to join these platforms and advertise their spaces. The platforms are also designed well as they both have good user interfaces that are easy-to-use for both the host and the tourist. There are subtle differences in the operations of both and this may give a clue as to the reason for Airbnb's success over that of HomeAway.

When it comes to guest fees, both platforms have decided to charge small guest fees. These charges occur in the percentage of the reservation amount. For pricing, HomeAway decided to opt for the simple pricing options. The company allowed the owners to sign up for a yearly annual subscription.

With Airbnb, the owners will be able to utilize pay per booking charge. Airbnb then charged a percentage of the host service fees. The company felt that the annual subscription charge option might not be viable for the host on a financial level. They felt that by charging fees on each reservation, they might get a lot of business.

They knew that with an annual subscription model, they would be able to keep the host on the platform for at least one year. However, the host may not even get one single guest that year and that might lead to a loss to the host. A loss only translates to poor feedback from the host (they might claim that the platform took the money without providing anything in return. Definitely not Airbnb's fault, but there is nothing to prevent such incidents from occurring). Airbnb clearly felt that while they might lose out or large revenues due to a subscription model, they might gain more loyalty through a reservation based pricing model. They understood that there are chances that the host may not want to maintain their subscription going into the next year.

Seems like their strategy worked.

The two companies also offer guarantees. Airbnb endorsed the Airbnb Host Guarantee program. That would provide protection against major forms of damage including theft, destruction of property or individual possession carried out by tourists. HomeAway caters to the guests with the Book with Confidence Guarantee. Though each has a guarantee program, due to the scale and capability of Airbnb, their program is more comprehensive when it comes to compensating negative events. From the evaluation,

HomeAway has a similarly elegant platform but is not at the same level as its main rival probably because it does not have the same network or innovative factors that allowed Airbnb to grow faster. Given a second chance, they may have done things differently to come up ahead.

VRBO for You?

Let's consider another example.

This one of VRBO, a company that was established in the 2000s. By the middle of the decade, they were able to amass over 65,000 properties across the country. Once they had acquired the properties, they realized that in order to expand, they would require a sizeable investment. Since they did not have the investment (and since they did not seek any financial influx), they decided to sell the company to HomeAway.

Leveling the Playing Field

With all this talk of competition, isn't there something everyone is forgetting? What about the fact that new competitors could come up? Should that pose a threat to Airbnb? What if someone else decided to launch a platform that has more innovative features than Airbnb?

Surely someone must have thought about it. They are probably waiting for the chance or collecting their investments as you read this line. Anytime now, they might make a move and dominate the market, ousting Airbnb as a leader.

While that might work well in theory, it might not be possible in reality.

You see, the plan has many pitfalls, and a lot of it has got to do with the properties that might need to come on board the system.

Let us look at the most obvious issues. The investment size needs to be large. This is because Airbnb already has a sizeable portion of the market. With that, it is not easy for competitors to try and enter the market because if they do, they might have two options:

- They use a small investment, in which case all that will accomplish is that they might end up being a small company. There are many Airbnb alternatives that you can find online with a smaller reach. A new company might end up becoming a part of this list of companies.

- Another option would be to outrank Airbnb. That means the new company has to have more listings on its platform than Airbnb. That would further mean that it would require a sizeable amount of investment. By that, I mean a really large investment to bring the company to the level Airbnb has reached now.

Another problem that the new company might face is the fact that it will need to get more people to sign up to this platform. You see, with all the features and benefits that Airbnb provides to its hosts, there is little chance they the same hosts will easily trust another platform. When they are used to one platform, it takes a lot of trust from their part to shift to another brand. Earning that trust is a long process. The new company might have to start from the bottom and slowly make its way up.

Now, this is assuming that Airbnb does not become aware of the new company. Obviously, anyone competing against Airbnb might come under its radar. They might monitor the progress of the new company.

If the new company rolls out a new feature, it will be far easier for Airbnb to adopt it quickly and launch it to the masses.

You might think that the ability to borrow features from another company does not easily happen, but you only have to look at the example of Snapchat and Facebook to understand why it is already possible.

You might know Snapchat as the platform that introduced the idea of sharing quick video messages between its users. You might also know that at one point, Snapchat was the only platform capable of providing this feature.

That soon changed in recent years when Facebook and Instagram both started providing the capability of creating short "stories", which are essentially Snapchat-like features.

In the world that we live in today, competition is high no matter what you do. Any idea can be easily adopted by someone else if you are not prepared for it. In this case, no matter which company starts to launch an innovative idea, Airbnb definitely has the advantage to roll it out faster. It might easily have gained popularity for the idea to such an extent that people might imagine that it was Airbnb all along who was responsible for creating the idea in the first place.

This does not mean that you cannot launch a company that can compete with Airbnb.

Far from it in fact. You can always make your presence known and be on par with Airbnb. However, you might have to go through cereal boxes for quite a few months. You might also have to face endless attacks from lawmakers, governments, city officials, and more. Then there are the problems faced on the platform with regards to the guests and the hosts.

With that, there are plenty of scenarios that you might have to face and your growth might take the course of years.

So yea, you have a chance indeed. But you might have to work really hard for it.

Chapter 5: Management Styles

Airbnb had made it. Despite many challenges faced during the journey of its growth, it has become the brand that it is today. One cannot look at an organization without trying to under a little more about it, particularly its management styles.

When asked about his management approach and the way it had changed over the years, Chesky compared the company to a big ship. As the chief executive, he likened himself to the captain of the ship, the only difference being that he had two jobs.

The first job that he had to pay attention to was where he had to worry about everything that is below the water. These are the factors that can sink the ship (his company, in other words). These factors include recent changes in law, situations that can cause harm to the company's reputation, the safety of the platform, and more.

The second job is the areas that he is passionate about, which include ways in which to improve the company. There are the main areas that can add value to the firm. These areas include the brand, the product and the culture.

When asked about how he approaches these two distinct jobs that he mentions, Chesky feels that he has a hands-on way of dealing with things. It is a strategic manner to approach management, one he feels fits well within the culture of the Airbnb organization.

Airbnb is not your typical organization. They do not publish an organizational chart. They do not explicitly have a diagram to show everyone the chain of command. However, they do place people in strategic positions in order to oversee different roles.

Numerous research conducted on the company shows that Airbnb is one of the few organizations that utilizes a holacracy type of system.

So time for another quick lesson.

A holacracy type of management is a form of decentralized management. This means that authority is distributed to each team and group within the organization. For example, let us assume that a company has a marketing department. Instead of directly managing the department, the marketing section is given a set of goals and the authority to achieve those goals in their own way. Of course, every task that they perform has to adhere to the company culture and established rules, but they have the freedom to work in a manner that they see fit.

Here is the breakdown of Airbnb's structure. There are 18 separate departments. The CEO is the representational head of the company, though he reports to the board of directors. Each of the departments come with a Vice President and each of those Vice Presidents report directly to the Chief Executive. So far, your typical organization.

It is under the departments of the company where things get a bit complex. Though the employees have the freedom to pursue their individual projects and ideas, they have to get approval from the supervisor of that department to make sure that it is in line with the corporate mission and the goals of the organization. Airbnb has product managers that also work in a lateral and horizontal manner with different departments. This means that each project manager works with the department he or she is responsible for and also provides assistance to other departments, should they require it.

For example, a design team may have a project manager, data scientist, engineer and researcher. The project manager makes the decisions on a day-to-day basis. He or she is responsible for getting the team to achieve their targets. While it is true that major decisions may need to be reviewed by the vice president in charge of that design team or perhaps even the chief executive, the daily operations are under the management of the team itself.

This sense of independence allows the team to achieve goals and even innovate in unique ways. It gives them the power to think outside the box, often coming up with surprisingly creative and different ways to handle a specific situation. In the end, that is what Airbnb aims for; to bring out the best way to manage different tasks and responsibilities.

The Hierarchy of Things

So that exactly does the hierarchy of Airbnb looks like?

There are at least five levels of hierarchy within the platform. The company has the top-level executive officers, who are directly below the CEO. They oversee a number of departments at the same time. Below them sit the Vice Presidents who are responsible for a specific department. Each department consists of a Product Manager/Department Manager and his or her staff. The levels would typically look like this:

CEO > Executive Officers > Vice Presidents or VPs > Product Managers/Department Managers > Staff.

Mentorship

Many members of the team receive mentorship. However, that is not restricted to just the staff. The founders also receive a lot of professional assistance from the outside to coach them on leadership.

In 2014, an external coach assisted Gebbia to deal with his perfectionist tendencies. This was addressed by making Gebbia come to the realization that it is okay for products to leave the door of the firm if they are less than perfect. The coach made Gebbia come to the realization that perfection is relative. Sometimes, it was necessary to have a higher emphasis on speed to ensure that the company can deal with certain situations in a timely manner.

Chapter 6: The Future of Airbnb

As a fortune 500 Company with billions of dollars, the question often arises about the firm in the next decade, 20 or even 100 years from now. Will there be an Airbnb, and will it exist in the current state with all the challenges and opposition that it faces? These are some of the questions that have been posed to the company founders.

Brian Chesky and Joe Gebbia have been quick to claim that the overall objective is to allow the company to endure even after they are gone. The mission objective of having a world where anyone can belong anywhere will the on the forefront of the company's mission no matter innovations arrive in the future. The founders hope that any changes or advancements that the company goes through in the coming years instills a sense of togetherness and reduces discrimination or sectarianism in any form or fashion.

Those are definitely lofty goals.

No matter how you look at it, the future is definitely an unknown factor in the company's growth, which is made more unclear with the number of challenges it faces today.

Since the time that it was just an idea, Airbnb has been at the forefront of the sharing economy. Even though millions of people list their homes on the platform and millions more use the platform for discovering short-term rentals, the growth has come under attack from regulations and rivalry. These factors clash with the freedom that allows renters to give out their space.

The founders have repeatedly reiterated that it is a currency of trust that represents the business when interacting online.

Airbnb provides an opportunity where the hosts can represent themselves as brands to the customers. This is the case in over 30,000 cities around the world except in countries like Iran, North Korea, Syria and Cuba. The founders claim the reason the company grew so fast is because unlike traditional firms, they were not building brick and mortar representations of the branches in every country or region.

They simply had people to represent them in various locations.

For example, the hosts in India provided the means to market the company in India. This made the Indian hosts Airbnb's branch in the Asian country.

In similar ways, it allowed its users to give it a sense of physical presence in every country that it operates in.

Togetherness

The culture of individualism has seeped through many areas of the world, including smaller communities, to the point where it is possible to be oblivious of one's neighbors even one's own apartment complex. Airbnb aims to create a disruption in this form of connectivity in a community.

Airbnb wants to change this perspective and have the sense of community brought back into the cities. Once people start to know each other, which sense of community would start to redevelop into what it once was. The idea of what a community once was harkened back to the days when people would give some of their time for their fellow neighbors.

When it comes to the nature of the city, Chesky did not want to avoid the urbane communities. He illustrates that it is not possible for the site to succeed without the use of cities. The goal is to thrive not just by having rentals in unique areas, but also in the cities where rentals can be accessible.

According to the founders, the goal for the future would be to have the cities embrace the sharing economy to new extents. They believe that fundamentally speaking, the ideology of the sharing economies is going to be beneficial for the city.

They believe that by providing people in any location to rent out their space, the company provides those people with the opportunities to become small entrepreneurs. This can get a little complex because there are regulations for people and those by which commercial enterprises run.

A Billion is Not a Big Number Right?

Airbnb would like to reach a place where they would be attaining as many guests as possible on their platform. But what do they mean by "attaining as many guests as possible?" That seems to implicate an arbitrary number. Are they looking for a million more guests? Tens of millions guests? 100 million perhaps? For any business, getting more customers is always the end goal. So what makes Airbnb's goal so high?

Apparently, Airbnb has a number and that dream number going forward happens to be a billion guests. That is right. Of course, that number does not mean that there will be a billion people making reservations. It just means that there will be a billion reservations made on the platform.

They have also charted a roadmap in order to reach this. One of the things that they are focusing on is the fact that they are introducing new types of rental spaces and property options.

The company is planning to introduce four new property modes that will be available for use.

These property options will include vacation homes, B&B boutiques, private rooms and shared spaces, and entire homes.

The company also plans to launch out special homes called Airbnb collections, which will be homes suited for any event. This means that if you have a certain event you want to hold within a space, you can rent out these homes for those reasons.

There will also be new categories offered to the users such as Airbnb Plus and Beyond by Airbnb.

Finally, in accordance with the mission objectives of the company, there will be regular community initiatives for corporate social responsibilities.

In a world that craves innovations, Airbnb is trying to step up their game so that they are the first to create something and the first to launch their creations in the market. While it is true that they do not have any competition currently, but that does not mean that the next would-be Airbnb would not arrive in the market with better features to offer.

Airbnb Collections

Remember the story of the nomads and the elderly couple who live in Airbnb homes? Well, it seems the company has taken some inspiration from it to create its new offering. Titled Airbnb Collections, these homes provide something more than the typical rental spaces. Up until now, Airbnb was designed for solo travelers (or even groups who are looking for small spaces). Over the years, the Airbnb community realized that they could use the website to get two forms of lodgings when they are travelling; the functional type spaces and the convenience based rental properties. That scenario is slowly changing. Now the platform can be used for families who want a space to cook and spend time together during their travels, or it can even function as layovers for honeymooners before they set off for their final destinations. For others, it can be a way to get off the beaten track. Airbnb had to diversify the usage of its homes in such a manner that it could then serve every type of traveler and customer. The company embarked on a campaign to launch Airbnb for work with collections adhering to honeymoons, weddings, family type of spaces and large groups who would like more facilities in their rentals.

Airbnb Types

The community offered is still very diverse at the present with nearly 4.5 million rental spaces to fill all over the world. These property types over the years have ranged from boutique hotels to tree-houses. However, regardless of the types of listings they have on their site, it is still possible to classify them into three forms.

These classifications would be shared spaces, entire homes and the private rooms. However, despite the multiple classification options available on the platform, some hosts are of the opinion that they are not allowed to stand out. And so, Airbnb has decided to add new types to the platform. These additions would be the vacation homes, B&Bs, unique space and boutique homes. This allows for a greater categorization option for the customers and gives the hosts a better means of expressing what they have to offer. This works particularly if what the hosts have is fits easily into the new rental spaces types instead of the original three options. It also gives better transparency on the accommodation modes. This is because the guests will automatically get a better understanding of the type of space they are about to rent. Additionally, these options might allow the hosts to better illustrate the unique selling points of their properties so that they can match the preferences of the guests. Airbnb has thus made the tools available to the guests in order to group themselves in a manner that fits them best. For example, are you a budget traveler or do you prefer boutique spaces? You can now easily classify yourself and find what you are looking for. Even within the travel sector, they can attract an even higher number of tourists who are aiming to have unique experiences that were not slotted in the primary property types.

Airbnb Plus and Beyond by Airbnb

Airbnb Plus was instituted to broaden the appeal of the platform in order to attract even more guests and to give recognition to the hosts. They wanted to motivate the hosts who try hard to give as much hospitality and high-quality service as possible to their guests. This new tier of homes on the platforms is those which have been verified specifically for comfort and quality. Beginning with 2,000 places in 13 urban areas that are available at the moment, plus it is meant for those guests that want the most exceptional hosts and additional verification on their travel. While some of these houses are already chosen by Airbnb to promote the service. These places represent the appeal of having the Airbnb stamp of quality on them.

To get a stamp of approval, a team from Airbnb will personally check and verify against a checklist that numbers from zero to a hundred (where zero represents the absolute worst in performance and 100 is the absolute best) on comfort, design and hygiene.

This comes with the already existing feature of providing the hosts with the label of "Superhosts, where the hosts have received great acclaims repeatedly by their customers in the reviews section.

With the Airbnb Plus feature, the hosts also benefit from top placement within the in-home services like expert photography and design consultation.

When it comes to Beyond by Airbnb, this is also another premier offering. Beyond by Airbnb is meant to provide custom designing trips for the customers on some of the best homes in the world. This is going to entail some custom experiences and world-class luxury. This is probably for the high-end clientele who are taking a liking to the platform and would like Airbnb to design an experience for them they would not have anywhere else. This improvement of the tiers section on Airbnb is a clear sign that the company is also venturing into the luxury department of travel where they will be catering to a select type of clients.

In fact, you can see this occur with the resort-like feel of Beyond by Airbnb. The characteristics of this package are similar to those of the high-end leisure lodging offerings in the market, but the difference with this one is it is being offered to a host of a smaller rental space than compared to a hotel.

This will soon evolve into the billionaire Airbnb package, where a customer who is a millionaire or has the temporary means can know what it is to stay in a billionaire villa, or a royal castle which is by the sea. Specific villas will gain attraction and the company expects there to be competition to get to stay at the front of the crowd. Airbnb feels that this is an option that will appeal to those would like to add a little more to their experience.

Success!

Airbnb is one of the biggest success stories there is out there. Three young men struggled against the odds and braved situations that would have made any lesser individual quit and look for an ordinary nine to five like everyone else. Instead, they took an idea which they were initially unsure of and they developed it until it became a company that has taken on a life of its own. There are several issues the company has had to contend with over the years, but these have served to make it stronger rather than affect its growth. When customer backlash against its handling of customer complaints became public, the company could have gone a very different direction. They could have cut losses and placed the blame on the customer when it suited them the most. It is quite true when people say that the company did not handle the situation in the best way at first. Considering the fact that the customer had to go public, which caused the company to lose face before they gathered their wits about them seemed like a terrible move at that time. However, they bounced back after the incident. They realized their mistakes and set about to correct them. They have also worked to regain and bolster the trust of the marketplace to a level they are considered a reliable member of the sharing economy, similar to other companies such as Craigslist and Uber.

This is because of the culture of trust which was built through ongoing consultation and referring to what the staff and their hosts need on the ground while providing an oversight authority to protect parties from damage in reasonable circumstances.

There have been issues encountered with the hotel industry/ however, that is something to be expected, especially when Airbnb graduated from the millions revenue bracket to the billions every year.

It has become evident they are stealing the market share from the vacations and hospitality industry using low prices and more reasonable conditions as related to the hotels which have enjoyed the monopoly on providing accommodations to travelers. The lobbying on the hotelier side definitely poised to discredit Airbnb in the market and make sure the company suffers legislative constraints in order to slow down their progress.

Unfortunately, it does not seem to be working fast enough because the platform is finding ways to outgrow the competition and soar to new heights.

If you look at how Airbnb managed to reach the point at which they are in right now, then you will notice a lot of factors that contributed to its growth. You might be aware of the fact that it had to go through numerous troubles during its initial phase. In fact, even getting an investor was a challenge to the team. Then there was the whole situation with the cereal boxes (they had to live on actual cereals for three months.) Then let's not forget trying to get people on board the platform and convincing them to stay there.

Of course, that happened with the founders actually reaching out to the user base and taking pictures of their apartments and rental spaces. All in all, it was a challenging growth phase for the company.

That being said, what really sets the company apart from the competition is the fact that its owners did not really have a lot of managerial or entrepreneurial experience. They had to learn everything as they built the company.

One can say that it is for this reason that they were able to tackle each problem as it appeared to them. It could also be the reason that the founders were able to use creative means to find solutions to many problems.

Right now, Airbnb is enjoying an incredible growth phase. It is sort of like teenagers have a growth spurt and finding out that they are among the tall kids in the class.

It definitely looks the same for Airbnb as well.

As a company grows, it is imperative that the founder or founders keep their goal in sight and think long term. With many companies that have risen to be on the same level of Airbnb, you often find the owners sell their company to another entity.

It happened with YouTube and it happened with Instagram as well. Those companies were bought by Google and Facebook respectively.

You see, Airbnb could have gotten down the same path. They could have sold their company ($38 billion is a lot of money) and made a huge profit out of it. But that is not the founders' intention. Chesky, Gebbia, and Blecharczyk are still in control of their company and are still leading it into new heights.

Look into many of the companies that you know today. Think if they have a trio of people who are leading it. In fact, take any example and you will find a solo entrepreneur or at most, a duo who manage the affairs of the company. The idea of three people still sticking together to manage a firm is quite unheard of.

Of course, the road has never been an easy one to follow. Especially when realizing that your company might have to come face-to-face with numerous governments around the world is enough to give one pause and think if it is all worth it pursuing the goals that they had set out to pursue.

Today, the founders are definitely tackling multiple roles. They are constantly learning new things. When faced with the situation where a single law can affect their business tremendously, Chesky, Gebbia, and Blecharczyk had to learn about the law and how to defend themselves against the opposition by themselves. Of course, they had a lot of help along the way. But that does not diminish the founders' interest in trying to learn about the situation. They did not choose to stay ignorant.

Then there is the idea of the business itself. You see, while their idea was actually simple, it was anything but when the time came to execute that idea. With an idea like Facebook, you have every aspect of its operation managed online. This is why it does come under such heavy scrutiny all the time. Sure, it has been subjected to questions by the government and other officials, but it does not face the opposition that Airbnb does.

With Airbnb, the concept is not restricted to just one platform.

It makes use of an online presence to stay connected with people around the world. But all the transactions, services, and experiences happen in real life. That is what sets the business apart from other companies.

Because of this dual aspect of making the business happen,

there were a lot more arrangements that needed to take place before the company took off. It is also the reason why there are many situations for the company to tackle when it comes to its processes. You have problems that occur within the system. These could include problems with the listings themselves payment mechanisms, glitches in the system, and other such problems with the platform itself. Then you have the problems that could occur in real life and these are the worst kind of problems. We have already seen what happens when guests destroy the property of the hosts and Airbnb's responses were not up to a good standard. We have already seen the extent to which lawmakers go to limit – and sometimes even ban – the services of Airbnb in their city or region. We have even seen the problems that hosts and guests can cause to each other. Each of these problems is not confined to a particular space. For example, they are not all happening online, where a few clicks of a button or a simple troubleshooting process can fix everything.

It is true, there are many companies who face the same type of risks. Think about companies like Uber who have to manage the various risks that it faces when it comes to its drivers. However, that does not diminish the challenges faced by Airbnb as well.

A key factor to remember about the founders was the fact that they were prepared to face the troubles head on. That is not something they knew from the beginning. That is an attitude that they picked up as they continued to manage the business.

Airbnb and its Customers

According to Morgan Stanley Research, it has been shown that the most important reason that people use Airbnb is because of the price options. Nearly 53% of the people who go on to the platform look for the price options on it and make a booking accordingly.

This is an understandable scenario. After all, if you are flying off to a place like Bali, then booking into a luxurious hotel or lodging is not the first thing that comes to your mind. In fact, it might not even be the second thing that comes to your mind. However, this begs the question, if the location is so important, then what is the point of giving all those extra features that we had noticed Airbnb was about to provide to its users?

There is one main reason for it; a higher profit margin. What Airbnb can earn by listing a condo that goes for $10,000 per night is easily more than 10 of the listings that is featured in the inexpensive room section. There is definitely money that the company can make through these special listings.

Here is another study that might interest you. In 2016, Cowen and Company discovered in their study that more than 90% of the people who have used Airbnb's services are satisfied by it.

This puts a whole new perspective on the company. When you understand that statistic, you realize that most of the problems that the company had faced fall into that 10% or so of the dissatisfied customers.

With Airbnb, the percentage of dissatisfied customers could have easily gone beyond even 20%. But the reason they are in the good levels is because they have maintained, for the most part, the quality of the services.

They have ensured that the customers receive the kind of satisfaction that they look for in the app.

However, that does not mean that they should not pay

attention to the 10%. Because even if one of those situations escalates into something serious, then Airbnb might have another fiasco on their hands something that they do not want to encounter during their growth phase.

This is something that the founders are all too aware of. They know the value of good customer service and after having experienced some extreme situations, they do not want to make the same mistakes again.

Another thing to ponder about is the fact that Airbnb is also popular with business travelers. These travelers claim that they are able to be more productive with many of Airbnb's listings. Now you might wonder how productivity is linked to homes. But here is what these travelers have to say about that.

They feel that the quiet atmosphere of homes are much better than the loud noises and the congestion one encounters in hotels. They apparently have a much better time getting their work done in such homes, especially if the homes also come with a kitchen.

Now, why are all these statistics important?

These stats show us that while the company has definitely faced challenges in the past, it is still a brand that has made its name in the minds of the people. It has created an impression that cannot be shaken off easily.

This is why officials, try as they might, cannot completely remove the presence of Airbnb.

While there have been measures taken against the company, pretty soon there will be some sort of leniency provided to allow Airbnb to function in many cities. This is because as public demand grows, so will the attention that the brand gets. As more and more hosts join the network, Airbnb receives even more influence. This cannot be ignored by lawmakers. If they do, it is like saying that they are choosing to ignore the voices of a million people who have been using Airbnb for a long time.

Here is Some Advice

The best advice that Brian Chesky ever got from that venture capitalist was to maintain the culture of his organization even when it seemed that compromise was inevitable. This is the overall thing which has strengthened and made the platform adaptable regardless of the attacks that have come its way. The reason is Airbnb culture is flexible and reasonable by nature. It focuses on the mutual benefit of all stakeholders and that is what a lot of companies do not understand. The company has made its interests synonymous with that of the employee and vice versa. It is only natural then that the employee would fight for the company's interests and bring in as much profit as possible. This has had an infectious effect as it trickles down to the hosts and even the customers. There is an air of professionalism and civility which is not contaminated by any corporate greed even though the financial benefit is a priority. Overall satisfaction for all participants is upheld.

The Three Musketeers

Usually, you will notice Brian Chesky and Joe Gebbia make public appearances for the company. They are certainly out there when they have to diffuse a situation or deal with opposition. This seems to put Nathan Blecharczyk in the backseat. However, his role in the company's functions cannot be underestimated.

You should know that much of what makes Airbnb a success is its technical aspects. While the service it offers and the features it provides to its hosts are important, none of them would be important if the website is not running smoothly or people are unable to use its features properly.

This is where the technical aspects of the website come into play. And the person responsible for these technical perfections is Blecharczyk.

In fact, most of the ideas of how Airbnb could grow without spending a dollar were conceptualized by Blecharczyk. It was his idea to use Craigslist to grow. It was also his idea to integrate the company with Google AdWords.

These little chances and recommendations definitely put the company on the map.

Additionally, it is only because the website is mostly running smoothly (mostly because no system is perfect. Even Google has been the subject of hacks and glitches) that people come back the platform and use it repeatedly. This is possible under the careful eye of Blecharczyk. Each of the founders contributes to the company in his or her way. They each have their strengths and together, they have managed to stay this long with the company.

Conclusion

There is much that goes into making a company.

There are challenges that appear unexpectedly and then there are problems that halt the progress of the company.

One thing to note is that no matter the situation, it is the leadership that is the guiding force of a company. In the case of Airbnb, all three founders have made it their mission to bring Airbnb to a level that is beyond even their expectations.

That is why Airbnb is one of the most incredible success stories of this generation.

Bibliography

Dominica | Data. (2019). Retrieved from https://data.worldbank.org/country/Dominica

The Great Recession. (2019). Retrieved from https://www.investopedia.com/terms/g/great-recession.asp

2015 in Review: Airbnb Data for the USA | AirDNA. (2019). Retrieved from https://www.airdna.co/blog/2015-in-review-airbnb-data-for-the-usa

The Great Recession's Impact on the Housing Market. (2019). Retrieved from https://www.investopedia.com/investing/great-recessions-impact-housing-market/

How 3 guys turned renting an air mattress in their apartment into a $25 billion company. (2019). Retrieved from https://www.businessinsider.com/how-airbnb-was-founded-a-visual-history-2016-2/?IR=T

The Poorest Countries in the World (2019-2023). (2019). Retrieved from https://www.focus-economics.com/blog/the-poorest-countries-in-the-world

Global Finance Magazine - The World's Richest and Poorest Countries. (2019). Retrieved from https://www.gfmag.com/global-data/economic-data/worlds-richest-and-poorest-countries

Airbnb: Advantages and Disadvantages. (2019). Retrieved from https://www.investopedia.com/articles/personal-finance/032814/pros-and-cons-using-airbnb.asp

(2019). Airbnb's CEO wasted weeks building a roommate-finding service before realizing it had already been done. Retrieved from https://www.businessinsider.sg/airbnb-ceo-explains-how-it-was-almost-a-roommate-search-tool-2015-11/?r=US&IR=T

AirBed And Breakfast Takes Pad Crashing To A Whole New Level. (2019). Retrieved from https://techcrunch.com/2008/08/11/airbed-and-breakfast-takes-pad-crashing-to-a-whole-new-level/

Obama O's: Hope in every bowl!. (2019). Retrieved from https://www.airbnb.com/obamaos

A short story about how Airbnb funded their startup with cereal boxes. (2019). Retrieved from https://medium.com/@austincoleschafer/a-short-story-about-how-airbnb-funded-their-startup-with-cereal-boxes-ac6e62cf4c4c

Combinator, Y. (2019). Office Hours with Michael Seibel. Retrieved from https://blog.ycombinator.com/office-hours-with-michael-seibel/

Gallagher, L., Gallagher, L., Kushner, D., Rosen, K., Rivlin, G., & Pontin, J. et al. (2019). Airbnb's Surprising Path to Y Combinator. Retrieved from https://www.wired.com/2017/02/airbnbs-surprising-path-to-y-combinator/

How Airbnb Founders Took Paul Graham's Advice to Heart. (2019). Retrieved from https://www.inc.com/abigail-tracy/how-airbnb-took-paul-grahams-advice-to-heart.html

Airbnb's co-Founder Joe Gebbia: "The World Thought We Were Crazy.". (2019). Retrieved from https://news.greylock.com/airbnb-s-joe-gebbia-the-world-thought-we-were-crazy-67d9269f55e5

'Airbnb mafia' fund Wave Capital makes it official, closing its debut fund with $55 million. (2019). Retrieved from https://techcrunch.com/2018/07/11/airbnb-mafia-fund-wave-capital-makes-it-official-closing-its-debut-fund-with-55-million/

Building a Strong Company Culture, with Airbnb CEO Brian Chesky. (2019). Retrieved from https://neilpatel.com/blog/brian-chesky-alfred-lin-culture/

Airbnb Finally Lands The Zappos Veteran It's Eyed For Years. (2019). Retrieved from https://www.businessinsider.com/airbnb-finally-lands-alfred-lin-2013-2/?IR=T

Primack, D. (2019). Early Airbnb investor resurfaces. Retrieved from https://www.axios.com/early-airbnb-investor-resurfaces-1513302675-c2f80162-4d62-44ea-93e6-032147bdd250.html

Airbnb's First Employees. (2019). Retrieved from http://www.firstemployees.io/company/airbnb

Airbnb report reveals Amsterdam rental levels and effects of new crackdown - DutchNews.nl. (2019). Retrieved from https://www.dutchnews.nl/news/2018/10/airbnb-report-reveals-amsterdam-rental-levels-and-effects-of-new-crackdown/

The Airbnb Effect: Cheaper Rooms For Travelers, Less Revenue For Hotels. (2019). Retrieved from https://www.forbes.com/sites/hbsworkingknowledge/2018/02/27/the-airbnb-effect-cheaper-rooms-for-travelers-less-revenue-for-hotels/

Airbnb horror stories: Ten times things went seriously wrong for hosts or guests. (2019). Retrieved from https://www.stuff.co.nz/travel/travel-troubles/104094634/airbnb-horror-stories-eight-times-things-went-seriously-wrong-for-hosts-or-guests

The Senior Nomads | Welcome. (2019). Retrieved from http://seniornomads.com/

Cullen, T. (2019). How Toshi Chan Went From Illegal Hotel Kingpin to Chelsea Hotelier. Retrieved from https://commercialobserver.com/2016/11/how-toshi-chan-went-from-actor-to-illegal-hotel-kingpin-to-respectable-chelsea-hotelier/

Deconstructing Airbnb's Full Value For Corporate Travel Managers. (2019). Retrieved from https://skift.com/2017/09/15/deconstructing-airbnbs-full-value-for-corporate-travel-managers/

www.ingramcontent.com/pod-product-compliance
Lightning Source LLC
Chambersburg PA
CBHW021820170526
45157CB00007B/2655